PRAISE FOR
THE WALL BETWEEN TWO LIVES

"A powerful book that gives hope during the most difficult times. Annette shares her self-healing journey in an authentic manner that will touch and inspire all. The consummate mentor, Annette has a passion for helping those around her and continues to do so through her memoir."

— Stephanie Brown
CEO and Founder, *The Rosie Network*

"Incredible story! Annette's ability to reveal her life, the highs & lows, really draws you in."

— Miller Browning
Founder of *Do Work That Matters*

"This book is the epitome of a ride through life. It's authentic and inspiring; packed with drama and conflict. The true elements of a hero's journey."

— Chris McPhee
Media Production Manager

"An extraordinary story of hope and true testament of inner strength, courage and determination! A must read for all!"

— Jillian Sandoval
Founder and CEO, *My Successful Future Inc.*

THE WALL

— BETWEEN —

TWO LIVES

A TRUE STORY OF FINDING PURPOSE

ANNETTE WHITTENBERGER

The Wall Between Two Lives:
A True Story of Finding Purpose

First Edition

Because of the dynamic nature of the internet, any web address or links contained in this book may have changed since publication and may no longer be valid.

The views expressed in this work are solely those of the author and do not necessarily reflect the views of the publisher, and the publisher hereby disclaims any responsibility for them.

Cover photo by Tara Ruby of Tara Ruby Photography.
Author photo by Chris McPhee of Green Beret Media.

Published by Tactical 16, LLC
Monument, CO

ISBN: 978-1-943226-60-3 (paperback)

CONTENTS

ACKNOWLEDGMENTS

This book would not be possible without God, my family, and my dearest friends.

DISCLAIMER: My husband did not want to be named in the book unless he was referenced as Remington J. Goldentuhle (all of the eye roll emojis). I would like to thank him for asking the hard questions and keeping me on my toes. He made me believe that this was possible. Although he did not want his name to be mentioned in this book, he is one of the reasons why I committed to my Army career. He saw the good, the bad, and the ugly and supported me anyway.

I would like to thank my children for loving me unconditionally through all the ugly parts of our lives. They are the most resilient, kind-hearted souls that I have ever met. I am the luckiest mom in the world and am so grateful that they chose me.

I would like to thank my brother for putting up with me through all of my life changes, mid-life crises, and terrible choices. Thank you for taking care of Mom while I tried to figure out my life.

Thank you to my mom for trying so hard to raise me through my stubborn and rebellious phases. Thank you for leaving your home in California to move to Texas so you could take care of our kids during our deployments. Thank you for always visiting us at each and every single duty assignment we were stationed at.

Thank you to those who believed in me throughout my life changes, career choices, and the journey that I felt I needed to go on. Thank you for pushing me to write this book and making me believe that I was made for more.

Thank you to my military family (including my peers, mentors, and leaders) for pushing me to continue through the ranks, no matter how difficult it was. Thank you for believing in me as a leader, mentor, peer, and friend.

Thank you to Brunella Costagliola of The Military Editor Agency for getting me started with your writing master class and pushing me to use my creative mind, and for making me believe in myself. Your lessons are how my journey took off, and I have never looked back.

Thank you to Chris McPhee of Green Beret Media for making me get out of my comfort zone when it came to sharing my story, using it on all platforms, and getting me in front of the camera. A HUGE thank you for introducing me to Tactical 16 Publishing. You know that we are just getting started.

A huge thank you to Chris Schafer of Tactical 16 Publishing for believing in me and my story. Thank you for accepting me as a writer and assisting me in bringing life into something that was previously merely words on paper. Your team has made one of my dreams come true, and this is just the beginning.

Thank you to my amazing editor, Jessica Reinken of Holistic Editing and Writing Solutions, who took the time to really get to know me and my writing style. She helped me in ways I never thought possible when it came to getting my voice heard through writing.

Last but not least, thank you to MG Dana Pittard (Retired) for writing the foreword of this book.

Thank you for starting the difficult conversation about depression from the senior leader's perspective. Thank you for believing in me and my work. You are the epitome of what we need in the United States military.

Without God, I would not be here sharing my message of hope. This is just the beginning, and I am so thankful to all of you for being with me on this wild ride called life.

FOREWORD

BY DANA J.H. PITTARD

I was both pleased and honored to be asked to write the foreword for this exceptional book. I have had my own personal challenges with mental health issues. I found that it was increasingly difficult in such a high-tempo and results-oriented organization like the US Military to ask or seek mental health treatment. Over the years, I have publicly and openly spoken of mental health treatment in an attempt to change the stigma of seeking help. We must look at ourselves as well as those around us who may be suffering from stress, depression, or other mental health problems. As a member of the board of directors of the Matthew Silverman Memorial Foundation for the prevention of youth suicides, I have worked to try to reduce suicides and promote mental health access.

I first met then-Major Annette Whittenberger when I was the commanding general of the US Army's 1st Armored Division and Fort Bliss, Texas (2010–2013). She was a very professional and dedicated Army officer. At the time, I did not know her personal story or the mental health challenges that she went through while balancing work, children, combat deployments, and being part of a dual-military couple.

As the commanding general of Fort Bliss, I saw firsthand the effects of years of combat operations on America's Soldiers and veterans. In 2010, Fort Bliss had one of the highest suicide rates in the Army. However, by 2012, Fort Bliss had one of the lowest suicide rates in the entire US Military.

The dramatic change in two years was due to a realization by the military leadership of Fort Bliss that anyone from the youngest Soldier to the most senior general officer could find themselves in a mentally "dark and painful place" and could consider taking their own lives to end the pain. The chain of command at Fort Bliss, in cooperation with the surrounding community of El Paso, developed over 30 initiatives to help identify and treat mental health issues.

This was the beginning of the highly successful No Preventable Deaths campaign at Fort Bliss. The underlying foundation of the campaign was a belief backed by data that if a person could be treated by mental health professionals, there was a greater than 90% chance of survival. The campaign included robust suicide prevention programs, the development of individual and collective resiliency, and an active attempt to de-stigmatize seeking help for mental health problems. In late 2012, I briefed President Barack Obama and members of the White House staff on the successful programs at Fort Bliss. Many of the successful lessons learned from Fort Bliss have been used throughout the US Army and the military.

After nearly 20 years of combat in Iraq and Afghanistan, like previous wars, the US military is not immune to mental health issues. Many of our veterans return from war with invisible wounds such as post-traumatic stress disorder (PTSD) or traumatic brain injuries (TBI). Annette Whittenberger has tackled many veteran mental health issues in her highly acclaimed podcast, "A Wild Ride Called Life." I was thrilled to be a guest on one of her podcasts. Her podcasts have helped many service members and veterans.

As Annette Whittenberger has noted, mental health can affect our daily living, relationships, and even our physical health. She has highlighted that mental health problems can be caused by stress, depression, anxiety, and other conditions. Seeking mental health treatment is often stigmatized in America and throughout the world.

In *The Wall Between Two Lives*, Annette opens up about her own individual battles with mental health while serving as a US Army officer. Her story is a powerful testimony of the need to de-stigmatize mental health care and to build a culture of seeking help. Her description of being sexually assaulted at the age of nine by the father of one of her best friends is heart-wrenching. Her determination and courage to testify against her assailant at such a young age are inspiring. She refused to be a victim and sought justice.

The Wall Between Two Lives is a deeply personal account of Annette's struggles with mental health problems caused by childhood trauma, sexual abuse, stress, depression, and other factors. Her story should resonate with both military and civilian audiences.

Annette writes:

> "What I have learned, several decades later, is that we all have a story
> to tell. We all have experienced some type of trauma in our lives.
> Throughout this book and through my story, you will see the many

phases of my life. What I want you to take from this is that I made it. I no longer live with the anger that I used to let consume me. I want my own kids to see that, even through the most difficult times, you can make it."

More than a mere account of her mental health challenges, *The Wall Between Two Lives* is a story of resiliency. At times, her story is raw with emotion, but that is how life can be at times. Most importantly, this is a story of triumph and hope. By telling her personal story, Annette gives hope to so many others who may be struggling with similar challenges. This is a compelling and important story.

— DANA J.H. PITTARD,
Major General, US Army (Retired),
Indianapolis, Indiana

THE WALL

BETWEEN

TWO LIVES

PROLOGUE

19 AUGUST 2018

IT WAS AROUND 9 A.M. on Highway 190 heading west towards Huntsville, Texas, when I was driving my daughter Haeli to college. This was about to be her first time away from home to live in a completely different state. She was going to be thousands of miles away from where our family was relocating to next, Northern Virginia.

It was like any other day with the sun out and a light breeze, nice enough to roll the windows down. It was almost calming as there were hardly any cars on the road. We had to stop at the nearest Sonic for one last time to get our large Route 44 drinks, cherry-flavored limeades with light ice, extra cherries, and vanilla syrup. It was one of our favorite drinks, and we weren't sure when we would even come across a Sonic again.

After grabbing our drinks, we started talking about how we were going to decorate her dorm room. Although I was a bit sad that I would no longer see her in her own room in our new house in Virginia, I could sense the excitement she had when describing how she wanted to decorate her new room. She said, "I can't wait to hang up those stringy lights around my bed that I saw at Target. Will you send me some, Mom?" I said, "Sure, once you find out what the rules are," since there were some guidelines in the welcome packet that she received. I could tell she was nervous because she started to play with her hair. "I spoke to one of my roommates, and we all agreed on what bathroom decorations we will be bringing with us so that it all doesn't fall on one person." I said, "Great. We can get them while we are down there." As she sat up in her seat, her eyes lit up, and she began to describe how she wanted her room to look.

Both Haeli and her brother Blaze were born in Hanau, Germany. Although I attended training in Germany earlier, Hanau was my husband and I's first duty station as a dual-military married couple. At the age of twenty-three and while being four months pregnant with Haeli, I moved across the ocean for the first time. It was a terrifying yet exciting time. It was Haeli and me from 2000–2003 until Blaze was born, as their dad would often have to leave on short deployments for work. Being a dual-military family would often require many sacrifices. His leaving for a brief deployment when Haeli was three months old was one of them.

As I listened to her tell me about the plans she had for her new dorm room, I couldn't help but think back to where the time had gone. It seemed like it was just yesterday where I would place her tiny little body into a baby carrier for the two of us to explore the downtown streets of Germany. Never did I realize that she would end up being my best friend.

"Mom, are you going to miss me?" she asked. I just kept staring at the road and said, "Duh." That was my way of shying away from talking about just how much I was going to miss her. She laughed a little and went through her playlist to find the next song to play. We turned up the music a little bit louder to keep our minds distracted. We didn't want to think about the fact that this would be one of our last road trips together for a while, and we just wanted to enjoy this time.

We were about an hour and a half away from one of the biggest moments of Haeli's life. "I am sad that dad wasn't able to come," she said. "I know, but you can Facetime him when we get there so that you can show him your room," I responded. "Plus, you can come home whenever you want — So we can look forward to that!" We were both a little sad that her dad and brother were not able to join us on this trip as her dad had work commitments and her brother had school. "Can you believe that I am going to be 18 in five days?" she said excitedly. "I know, and I am so sorry that we won't be there to celebrate with you," I said. My sadness was as clear as day in my tone, even though I was trying hard to conceal it. "It's OK, Momma. My new friends and I already talked about what we are going to do," she said with a smile. I knew then that she was going to be OK. My big girl was going off to college. She was off to be the independent and sassy girl that we had raised her to be.

Suddenly, I saw something odd in the corner of my eye. Something in front of me. Something that wasn't supposed to be there.

A red car?

"MOM!"

That was the last word I heard before impact.

———

On August 19, 2018, at approximately 9 a.m. CST, a car with two women, approximately 40 yrs old (driver) and 18 (passenger), driving on Highway 190 toward Huntsville, Texas, was struck head on by another car driving in the opposite lane.

Paramedics and police officers are on the scene.

The conditions of the two women (victims) are unknown, as paramedics are struggling to get them out of the car, which on impact has rolled multiple times and turned upside down.

We will keep you updated once we receive more information.[1]

1   Polk County Publishing Company. "Six Injured in Multiple-Vehicle Crash." Tyler County Booster, August 27, 2018. https://www.tylercountybooster.com/index.php/news/2447-six-injured-in-multiple-vehicle-crash.

1: FALL IN

Fall in — to take one's place in a military formation or line;
"Troops fall in!"[2]

1981, SIMI VALLEY, CALIFORNIA

I WAS SIX YEARS OLD when my world was first turned upside down. I had to learn how to fall in, grow up, and move on.

"Daddy, are we going back to the Circus Circus Hotel next time we come visit?" I would ask my father on the alternate weekends we spent with him. My parents divorced when I was six years old, and my younger brother Oscar and I often looked forward to any trips that my dad had planned during his visitations. "Yes, Pumpkin Nose!" he said, looking down on me as he patted my head. He often called me "Pumpkin Nose" because he said that when I was born, my nose looked like a little pumpkin.

I remember visiting my dad every other weekend after the divorce. We would take trips to the Circus Circus Hotel in Las Vegas. The hotel was bigger than anything that I had ever seen. I remember walking in with my eyes wide open and mouth practically to the floor. My eyes were blinded by all the lights, and my ears were ringing from the sounds of the other children's laughter and noises from the games. Oscar and I used to play for hours until our coins ran out.

THE WALL BETWEEN TWO LIVES

We would pile into our dad's small truck that had a camper on top. It was a late-1980s truck that was white with light blue stripes. My brother and I would take naps on what seemed like a mini bunk bed in the back of the trailer. We thought that it was the coolest thing ever; we felt like big kids. That truck gave us many memories, the other ones being our trips to Tijuana, Mexico, back when it was safe. We would always get homemade tamales from the locals who would practically be waiting for us at the border. I remember walking the streets, looking at all the beautifully colored Mexican pottery, and eating fresh tortillas. I ended up returning later on while I was in college.

The shuffling between two parents every other weekend was hard on all of us, but those memories of our trips to Las Vegas and Mexico are the ones that stick out the most, as if it all just happened yesterday. We didn't focus on the fact that our parents were divorced. As young kids, we just wanted to know when the next trip was and where. The fact that we had bedrooms in two separate houses did not seem like a big deal until we were much older. It just seemed like an adventure. My parents lived in the same small city, about fifteen minutes away from where my mom had purchased the other house where we would call our new home. It did start to seem strange that my father had stayed in the house that we lived in first, but I don't remember asking any questions, nor do I remember any of the feelings that went with my parents parting ways. I blocked this part out to protect myself and my brother from what would lie ahead. Moving in with my mother seemed so final, but Oscar and I were still left with so many unanswered questions.

My mom both worked a full-time job and attended college at California State University Northridge to complete her bachelor's degree. I remember how stressed out she was while trying to raise my brother and me. Although I felt like we grew up a lot quicker than some, what she tried to instill in us would make much more sense later on in our lives. When we moved into our new house, she told us, "I am going to need your help now that it is just the three of us." Oscar and I looked at each other with that confused glare, never really understanding what those words would entail.

My brother and I grew up as latchkey kids because our mom had no other choice. We would walk to and from school or take the bus on our own. We would come home, get a snack, then do our homework. The food combinations that two kids home alone could come up with were priceless. I discovered that drinking dill pickle juice was a lot tastier than I had anticipated. Before you roll your eyes, have you even tried it? That bitter taste in the liquid was almost as refreshing as a glass of lemonade. My friends thought I was so bizarre, but if you are an avid fan of dill pickles, this is the drink for you. We also discovered things like eating cold mash potatoes with barbecue sauce, and butter and sugar sandwiches. Although butter and sugar sandwiches didn't stick with me into my adult years, the mashed potatoes with barbecue sauce is still a favorite today. You are probably reading this thinking, "What the hell?" and either snickering or laughing because it sounds gross or you can actually remember eating all kinds of similar and ridiculous things.

———————

The 1980s was an epic era.

At my mom's house, one of the spare bedrooms was converted into our TV and game room, which always remained locked until she gave us permission to enter it. She was that mom who would literally check the TV's temperature by placing her hand on the back to see if we turned it on or not. Going into that room was forbidden, and we were deathly afraid that she would catch us... well, kinda.

She said, "You are not to watch any television until I say it is OK, and I *will* find out," while looking at us with that look that would terrify any kid. My brother and I would look at each other in fear and just nod our heads in agreement. There were a couple of rules that we knew we had to abide by. One of them was to not enter the TV room, and the second was that no one else was allowed into the house when she wasn't home. Somehow, we still pushed the limit and figured out a way to sneak into that room. Even though I think she knew, we would still go in there. There were times when I could estimate when she was due to arrive home. I would watch to see when her car was coming down the street, and then I would yell to Oscar, "Hurry up, Mom is almost home!" We would rush to turn off the TV, shut the door, run to our rooms, and pretend as if nothing had happened. As long as we didn't break into a full sweat or make it obvious that we were guilty, she didn't check that room, but, boy, were we close. Although my brother and I were fearful of our mother, we were kids who still liked to see what we could get away with.

Thinking back to my childhood, I am not sure how we got away with the things we did since our mom was so strict — like, the scary kind of strict, with eyes growing in the back of her head. She was that one who threw the *chancla*, also known as whatever shoe she had access to, and she never missed a shot. She would grab anything that was the closest to her and throw it at us when we got her angry enough. It would often rotate between the chancla, spatula, hairbrush, or a pan. And, no, we didn't get to pick. She was definitely the disciplinarian that shook us to our core.

As I grew into my teen years, I have to admit that I did take advantage of my dad not being the disciplinarian. Whatever my mom wouldn't let me have, I would ask my father for. It started with a phone in my bedroom. It was not anything fancy, just one of those infamous banana-shaped ones with a long, twirly cord and beige color. Somehow, I was able to talk my dad into convincing my mom to let me have one. I mean, all my friends had one, So why not? I knew I could ask him for things that I could not ask for from my mother.

The next, most significant thing that I asked for was a car. So, with help from my mom, I started working at the age of thirteen. My mom specifically stated, "I will get you whatever you will need for school, but all the extra stuff that you want, you will have to save up and pay for." I was so bummed but replied with "Yes, Mom," while rolling my eyes and thinking how unfair it was.

I ended up working throughout high school while also studying, playing in some sports, and being a cheerleader. I remember going into my first real job at a local Ralphs supermarket — I was nervous, afraid, and, yet, a little excited to be able to get this experience. I walked in with sweaty palms and my stomach in knots, not knowing what to expect. Those of us who were hired were there to assist with opening a new store in the small community called Wood Ranch. This was my first real job that didn't require help from my parents (as opposed to the job I had at thirteen). I had no idea how I was going to juggle it all at the age of sixteen. How did we kids at that age even handle the stress?

I worked several jobs throughout high school so that I could afford my first car. My parents and I agreed that we would all contribute to the purchase. Because my father had experience with cars, he was able to find me a black 1981 El Camino. Can you even imagine me driving it? A young, sixteen-year-old girl driving an El Camino? It was surely not something I would have picked out, but I trusted my mechanically inclined father's reasoning. He actually owned a mechanic shop that specialized in FIAT® cars, So why wouldn't I have trusted his judgment?

I am sure my friends from high school, who are probably reading this right now, are laughing to themselves because they remember the car that pretty much stood out like a sore thumb. I thought it was so cool because it had an alarm system. I am actually laughing as I write this because the alarm would randomly go off during class. I would have to leave class to shut it off. I was so embarrassed. The car, unfortunately, didn't last long. I would be lying if I didn't say that I was both a little sad and relieved that I had to let the car go.

Next car... a maroon 1983 Ford® Mustang with silver rims. Let's just say that this car didn't last very long either. Having a father as a mechanic should have taught me a few things, but instead, I acted like an irresponsible teenager.

What had happened was... I had gone out with some friends and was late for my curfew. As I headed down the freeway and exited the off-ramp, my car started to smoke. I pulled over to the side of the road, got out of the car, and noticed liquid coming from the undercarriage of the car. I knew that I was in trouble.

You may be asking about how the hell I caused my car to spring a leak. All I can say is... I don't even know. I didn't check the oil like I should have and ignored the check engine light. That damn light always came on, and I never knew when it was serious. So, I blew it up, thus setting a personal record by going through two cars within a year and a half.

This time, we went for a 1994 white Honda Civic hatchback from a dealership, thinking that, maybe, I would have better luck with a newer car. This purchase actually lasted for more than a few months, but I got screwed over in the price that I paid. As a first-time buyer under the age of twenty-five, I spent a ridiculous interest fee of 21 percent. Don't even ask. In fact, as proof, I found that yellow piece of paper a few months ago. I will keep it forever as a reminder of that time.

That Honda lasted me ten years, and it was a great car. She even went with me to my first duty station and survived the Autobahn of Germany. If you have never driven the Autobahn, then you might not know that the speed limit was pretty much whatever you wanted. No joke. It was regulated in certain areas, but, for the most part, you could never outrun the Germans who were often going at least 100 mph.

We had a great run until I became pregnant with Haeli. It was apparent I wasn't able to fit into that car anymore. I would have had to literally have to roll in sideways. As much as I wanted to fit a car seat in the back, that car was just not going to cut it as a little family car. It was so hard to let that car go, but she found a new home with a young soldier.

The fourth car was never expected and quite surprising, a Dodge Caravan. It all started with my husband saying, "I found the coolest van, and it's silver!" OK... Wait a minute. "Cool" and "van" do not belong in the same sentence. Are you laughing? Because I wasn't. In my head, I was wondering, What in the world was my husband thinking!? I never wanted to be labeled as a "soccer mom" at the age of twenty-five. After he explained to me why he thought that it was a good idea, I have to admit that it made sense. I was literally growing out of the Honda. We knew that we wanted more than one child, so the van would make more sense to fit multiple car seats, strollers, groceries, and other passengers when family came to visit.

I was a little sad because I really wanted a BMW station wagon. They were fairly inexpensive, especially in Germany. But, he was right, the station wagon would not make sense for what we would need it for, so the van it was. Back in 2000, most vehicles were still standard. There were no power windows or seats. They didn't have bucket seats that were easy to take in and out. The Caravan was the most standard van you could find, and it brought our family so many memories.

The funny thing is that we still own that van to this day, making her over twenty years old. We carried both of our children in her. At one point, I had the windows tinted to try and make her look "cooler." We traveled across Europe with her. She has been in car accidents, The Autobahn, and DC traffic. She has broken down, had parts replaced, and, at one point, we thought we were going to lose her. She is part of our family, and it has been a struggle to let her go. We know that our family will be her final destination, and we are actually trying to prepare ourselves for it. The van that I never thought I wanted is now something I never knew I needed. I never understood why separation from people or even materialistic things were so hard for me until I looked back at my childhood.

I think my dad felt that letting me have the little things I asked for could make up for him not being as present in our lives as we wanted him to be. By asking for and receiving stuff from my dad, it was almost like a way of getting his attention and filling a void that I didn't realize I needed to be filled. This feeling ended up becoming a big part of me throughout my life as I struggled in my relationships. I had anger and resentment that I never knew how to really deal with.

After I was well into my teenage years, visitation with my dad slowly started to become less frequent. Something always came up, and I began to feel less connected. My dad wasn't around much when I had sporting events or when I wanted to show off my school report card. I did not have him around to talk about dating or boys, and it was a feeling that was often difficult to just push aside. I was starting to grow up way too fast, and he was missing it all.

"Dad, why can't you come to get us this weekend?" I would ask him when he called to tell Oscar and me that he couldn't come. "It will be soon. I just need to take care of some things," he would reply, always delivering vague answers that would often leave my brother and me sad and confused. I quickly learned that we would see him when we could and that we just needed to continue to live our lives. I knew that our dad loved us. I just learned that, sometimes, love is hard to express.

I noticed that things started changing when I was around ten years old. This was when my first step-brother Chris was born. My second step-brother Carlos was born when I was thirteen years old. Rather than being upset that my dad had another family now, I was a little excited to get to know these two new additions. As they grew older, I started seeing so many similarities that would bring us closer. They began to take on the same personality and the same features as my father and my other brother. They had that quirky sense of humor. They always seemed to find humor in everything and never really took anything too seriously. Life changed drastically as they moved several more times, and I did not get to see them again until they were in their teenage years.

I feel as though the addition of having two more brothers has somewhat saved what is left of my relationship with my father. Knowing that there were two other people involved in our lives made it that much more important to me to keep whatever was left in our relationship. I grew to stop being angry with my father for not being as engaged in our life as he should have been, and I tried to create a relationship with his sons. To me, that's what was now important. I wanted them to know that they had a family. I was now the big sister and the only sister that they had. All the anger I had been keeping inside was now turning into wanting to better my relationship with this other part of my family. I couldn't move on knowing that there were two other lives out there that were carrying our last name. I love my father and always will. He is my dad. All of his boys and I are just like him. From facial features to personality, we are all very similar. There are things that will never change. There are also things that I wish I could have changed, but that is not what I wanted to focus on anymore as I slowly learned that I needed peace.

Growing up with divorced parents is not something I have ever taken lightly. Even though it was just considered normal for me since the age of six, it did impact me. There were moments where I would be lost in thought about how my life could have been different. I wish my children would have had my father, their grandfather, in their lives, but it didn't happen that way, and not talking about it was how I dealt with it. I acted as if having divorced parents was not a big deal. Yet it really was.

I felt like I had spent my life trying to heal a broken heart. I poured myself into other things to mask how I truly felt. I found myself drowning my feelings in retail therapy, emotional eating, and hoarding. I didn't know how to let go. Part of me still doesn't know how. I have been struggling with this all my life, and to actually write this is all part of my journey. As I sit here reading this, I now feel like I can breathe a little bit easier. It is not easy to admit why you think you turned out a certain way when you have been hiding from it all your life.

As a parent now myself, I have had to make choices for my own family. Some of those choices were learned from my own parents. Some are a result of how I was raised. Some are from my poor choices and not knowing how to properly deal with certain situations in my life. These were the hard choices that I had to make to have peace in my heart. It took me years to get to this place. There are still days where I question a lot of the choices I have made, but I have now learned how to have some grace within myself.

How I lived my life from age six until now was not something that I had planned. My life is drastically different from how I had imagined it would be. I have turned my messes into messages, and I hope you will see how and why I have chosen to do so. What I have learned, several decades later, is that we all have a story to tell. We all have experienced some type of trauma in our lives. Throughout this book and through my story, you will see the many phases of my life. What I want you to take from this is that *I made it*. I no longer live with the anger that I used to let consume me. I want my own kids to see that, even through the most difficult times, you can make it.

Although I wish that my father would have been more present in my life, I also wish that I would have been closer with my immediate family on both of my parents' sides. I didn't get the chance to grow up with cousins and grandparents, and it sucked. Later in life, I found myself really missing the fact that I didn't have the same memories with my grandparents as some of my friends did with theirs. Hell, I was even jealous of my own cousins, who were able to grow up with our grandparents. Like other families, ours, too, was a complicated one. Our family had secrets and held grudges that lasted for decades. It was not something that any of us could change, and none of us wanted to be stuck in the middle of it. I had to learn to focus on all the positive things that I learned during my childhood. I pushed the sadness aside and taught myself to be tougher... or at least that's what I thought I was doing.

I used my relationships as lessons for something better and more meaningful later on in life. It was important to me to show my kids that family can be complicated, but family can also be the ones that we rely on the most. There is no handbook on how to deal with family. There is also no handbook to teach you how to be a parent. We continually try to raise our kids the best way we know how, regardless of how we grew up.

So, how would you have dealt with this type of family dynamic? There are many scenarios, many ways that this could have turned out. I had to choose to let go. I never wanted to relive the day that my parents no longer lived in the same house. I never really spoke about it with my dad. I kind of just looked past it because I think part of me never really wanted to know. Because my mom was still bitter about it, there were times where her anger would turn into lashing out with negative words about my father. It was a constant battle to hear the arguments between the both of them. As a child whose parents went through a non-amicable divorce, you hear and see things that you try to ignore. I didn't know any other way to deal with it but to decide not to take sides. From an early age, I started to learn how to suppress my feelings to try and please others. Was that the right answer? Some may say, "Absolutely not."

WHAT WOULD YOU HAVE DONE?

For me, there was no right or wrong answer. I loved my parents, but I didn't know what else to do. One of the hardest things to witness was the relationship between my brother and our dad. They no longer have a relationship; to this day, it breaks my heart. There is nothing I can do or say to resolve it. The relationship between the two started drifting apart during the end of our high school years, and the phone calls no longer came as frequently. I would be lying if I said that seeing my dad miss out on my wedding, my brother's wedding, and my brother and I's kids growing up didn't tear me apart. I have seen the relationship between our father and us completely fall apart because of broken hearts, anger, and pride. There are so many things that I can equate this to, but, nonetheless, our family was broken, and I saw it break first-hand.

Oscar and I are now in our forties and have learned how to continue on with our lives in the best ways we can. Some days are better than others, but the one thing that we do have is each other. My brother and I are very close and have stated that we will not let anything get in the way of our lives, especially with our kids. A part of me is still hurt, and I still get sad. Another part of me is just glad that my father is still around for his other two boys and grandson. At least he is still here. I am grateful for that.

I write this and share this part of my life because it has taken me years to try and come to terms with it. My dad is a good man. He has a good heart. He made mistakes, but haven't we all? I just think about all the mistakes I have made that have destroyed lives, including part of my own. Who am I to live in judgment?

I feel that he has some internal struggles that he never learned to cope with. I have also learned this about my mom. Their generation didn't talk about their feelings, and that was passed down to us. It was just "the thing to do." I am not saying that it is right. I am saying this because I have found out that others my age, who grew up in the late 1980s, state the same thing. Once we start talking about our childhood, we end up nodding our heads and saying, "Oh my gosh, yes! I can totally relate." It is a sad reality, but learning to acknowledge this issue is the first step to healing. We have to make the conscious decision to teach our kids not to do the same thing. As hard as it was for me to learn how to communicate, I knew that it would be one of the most important things that would save my life.

As you will see throughout this book, it took me a very long time to learn how to use my voice. It was a challenge, a struggle, and one of the hardest things that I have had to learn how to do.

So… here we go.

> *Dear Dad,*
>
> *If you are reading this, please know that I do love you. I forgive you, and I want you to be at peace. You and Mom brought me into this life, and I will forever be grateful. Take a deep breath, and know that you are reading something that only a strong person could write. I am going to be OK.*
>
> *Love,*
> *Pumpkin Nose*

For my readers, I challenge you to dig deep and accept the place you are in. You were made for more. *Your mess is your message*, and you are still here for a reason — no matter how your life is turning out.

2: DRESS RIGHT, DRESS

Dressing. Right Dress, — all personnel except the right marker bring up their left arms parallel to the ground.[3] The platoon is aligned in basically the same manner as the squad. On the command of execution DRESS of Dress Right, DRESS, the first squad leader stands fast and serves as the base. Other squad leaders obtain correct distance by estimation.[4]

19 AUGUST – 25 SEPTEMBER 2018, CONROE, TEXAS

On Monday morning at approximately 9 a.m., the Texas Department of Public Safety troopers responded to a four-vehicle crash in US-190 in Tyler County, which occurred near CR 4040.

Initial reports indicate that a 2003 Jeep was traveling eastbound on US-190. A Honda passenger vehicle was traveling westbound on US-190 followed by a 2017 Jeep and a 2009 Dodge Ram pickup truck. For an unknown reason, the driver of the 2003 Jeep crossed the center dividing line and struck the Honda. After colliding with the Honda, the Jeep then struck the 2017 Jeep and continued off the roadway. The impact of the second collision caused the 2017 Jeep to collide with the Dodge pickup truck.

The driver of the 2017 Jeep, 43-year-old Annette Whittenberger of Killeen, was transported to Conroe Regional hospital with unknown injuries. Her passenger, 17-year-old Haeli Whittenberger, was transported by ambulance to a local hospital in Lufkin with serious injuries.[1]

WHAT I JUST SHARED with you above comes straight from the Tyler County Booster online source. What I will share with you next will be straight from memories that will never go away. The forthcoming details changed the next phase of my life. What I hope you gather from the details is that trauma affects everyone differently, but it does not define you.

Why did I put this in Chapter 2? Well, why make you wait until the end of the book? Kind of cruel, right? I placed this here so that you can see what changed me at a time when I thought I was lost. As you read the rest of this book, you will see accounts of what I felt was very impactful in making me who I am. At this point in my life, I felt as though everyone else was in the Dress Right, DRESS. I felt like I was left to make room in the formation, also known as the rest of the world.

———

Here we go.

My eyes opened, bringing me to realize that our rental 2017 Jeep was upside down. I felt like I could not breathe, but I tried to remain calm as I looked over at my daughter. Our Jeep had rolled over. Haeli was in the air with her seatbelt being the only thing holding her in. She immediately started crying and screaming, "I can't feel my leg." I took a deep breath and assured her as confidently as I could, "It is going to be OK. Just breathe." I still don't know how I kept it together. Maybe I was in shock, but in my mind, I was thinking, "Holy shit — what just happened?" My chest was tightening up from the impact of the airbag. My left arm was hanging outside of the broken window. I looked over to see that there was a piece of glass stuck in my left middle finger. I so badly wanted to rip it out. I even tried leaning over to take it out, but I was strapped in so tightly that I could not move. I noticed blood on the window and looked around to see where it was coming from. I looked back over at my left forearm and saw that it had broken through the shattered window during our rollover. I was so focused on Haeli that I was not able to see that my forearm had been completely sliced open. In fact, I was starting to lose feeling on my whole left side. I felt this huge wave of panic but could not show it as I needed to remain calm for my daughter.

People started showing up around the car. I do not know if they were bystanders or if they were first-responders. I could not see past the inside of the vehicle. I remember slowly repeating, "Lord, please help us," while thinking of all the times in my life where I should have prayed to God. Why would He help us now? I was raised Catholic. Throughout my life, I lost and found my way several times. I know that I did not pray or thank God for my blessings as I was raised to do. All I know is that at this place in time, right here in this moment, I needed God to keep us alive. I started to relive moments from months prior when I contemplated ending my life because I wanted the pain to end. I realized then that I actually did not want to die. I wanted to live. I wanted to be here, and I was begging Him to honor that just this one last time.

Someone came to my window. My heart was racing, and I immediately started breathing very heavily. I thought, "Oh no... not a panic attack, not now." It is almost like I needed permission to let all of my emotions go. I was trying so hard to remain calm, but inside I was freaking the hell out. It felt like a nightmare, and I wanted to scream. One minute we were on the road laughing and listening to music, and the next, all I heard was "MOM!" in Haeli's terrified voice.

He came out of nowhere. I could not have done anything to avoid that 2003 Jeep as it slammed into us head-on at full speed (by the way, the speed limit was 65 mph, and we all know that people don't pay attention to that number). Now, here we were, in the rental car, upside down, trying to comprehend what exactly got us here. I remember getting hit and losing control of the car. I do not remember flipping or anything else after that.

A stranger came to my side of the car, knelt on the ground, then asked if we were OK. She said not to worry and that help was coming. She then asked who she could call. I was surprised that I could remember phone numbers. I am sure if someone were to ask you for a phone number, there may be just a few that you could remember, right? We are so used to our phones storing every bit of information that if we were to lose it, we may very well be shit out of luck.

I gave her my husband's phone number first, hoping that he would answer but was not surprised when he didn't. He usually leaves his phone by the couch when he is working on something. I was not even angry. I sighed and gave her my son's phone number next. I was shocked that I could remember that one as I was prone to mixing up the last four digits of his phone number quite frequently. My son didn't answer his phone either. Blaze later remembered seeing a text from an unknown number. After reading the text, he called the lady back. Blaze then notified my husband that Haeli and I were in a car accident.

This kind lady then asked if she could pray with me. I had not prayed in so long. I didn't even feel right about it. I started to hear other voices surrounding the car. I even heard someone say that they needed to hurry because they smelled gas. I closed my eyes as she prayed. I felt useless. I could not get out. I could not help my daughter. All I could do was hope that God was listening to this stranger as she prayed. More people started to surround us. I kept hearing voices from different people. I kept hearing the sirens of the ambulance and the helicopter's whirling blades.

Things started to happen quickly.

A man came over to me and tried to explain what the next steps were going to be. I immediately told him that I did not want to die. He said that he was not going to let that happen. I felt the tears falling from my eyes but knew that this was not the time to break down. I needed to be strong. He explained that there was no way for me to get out of our Jeep unless they took the hood off of the car. He told me that he would be putting a cloth over my face so that debris would not get into my eyes. My heart was racing. I was terrified, realizing how bad this situation really was.

The medics took Haeli out first. I could hear her screaming. She was so scared and in so much pain. She kept asking about me, and all I could do was wait until I was also taken out. I hated that I could not directly be there for her. I hated that she was in pain, but I was also glad that I was in worse shape than she was. I would never want anyone to endure what I was going through at that very moment.

I could hear the loud noise of the extraction tools they were using to cut the hood off. What probably took only minutes felt like forever as I waited to be taken out of the vehicle. As soon as the jaws of life lifted that entire hood from above me, I could see the light. It felt like there truly were lights at the end of this tunnel, but it would take months before I could truly appreciate what that truly meant.

I was finally taken out of the vehicle with precise movements as no one knew the extent of my injuries. I was placed on the ground and then eventually onto a gurney. As I was lying on that gurney, I started to panic. In the back of our Jeep were all of my daughter's belongings that we were taking to her dorm. I did not know how much was lost. I did not know what would be happening to the vehicle (or, at least, what was left of it). I just knew that I needed someone to find my bag with all of her important documents and my phone. If anything, those documents needed to be saved, and I felt like I could not leave the scene without them. One of the most surprising things to me was that my phone had no damage. It may seem trivial, but that LifeProof case that I invested in saved it, and, to me, that was a sign of what was to come next.

To my knowledge, my husband called my father-in-law immediately to notify them of my daughter's location. As we would soon find out, her destination would not be the same as mine. I was so confused, delirious, heartbroken, and in pain that I didn't know where she was going until I was already in the helicopter. I was being taken to Conroe Regional Medical Center, which was about a twenty-minute flight from the accident. She was taken by ambulance to a hospital that was much closer because her injuries were not as serious as mine. She ended up with a broken left leg, requiring her to have a life-long titanium iron placed in there for stabilization. We were very fortunate that both my father- and mother-in-law were able to make it to the hospital in time to be there as soon as Haeli was out of surgery. When I found that out, I knew that she would be OK. I was relieved to know that she was not alone.

As soon as I arrived at the hospital, I had so many people around me, all working on me at the same time. I couldn't focus. I kept asking for my daughter. I needed someone to make sure I knew where she was and if she was OK. The nurses started to cut off my sandals because my toes were broken. I remember pressing down on the brakes in full force at impact. Because I was wearing sandals, they were not protected.

They proceeded to take off all my jewelry, including my "mom" necklace that my kids gifted me about five years prior. I started to panic and told them that I couldn't take it off. I never take it off. My kids bought this for me. I felt like I was hyperventilating. They assured me that it would all be kept with the rest of my things.

I can't clearly remember what happened next except for waking up in the hospital room after surgery. I was in so much pain and didn't know the extent of my injuries until the doctors came in to tell me:

- I had broken my left arm, causing them to have to put in plates and screws.
- There was nerve damage to my entire left forearm due to the window glass puncturing and slicing it open.
- There was minimal damage to the inside of my right forearm, which caused numbness from the elbow down.
- I lost full mobility of the thumb on my left hand, which has yet to regain mobility to this day.
- The left side of my hip was permanently damaged, requiring a hip replacement less than a year after the accident.
- My left thigh was damaged from impact, causing me to lose about 80 percent of any feeling in that leg.
- My left calf and ankle will forever have plates and screws in them, also leaving me with very minimal mobility and feelings of numbness.

I required a total of six surgeries and a blood transfusion. Even after all of that, I fully tried to appreciate that I had no internal bleeding or brain damage. I can still say that things could have been worse. Looking at my scars now, I can see a story of survival and of pain. Although I can honestly say that I hate those scars, I know that they tell a part of my story.

I spent the next five weeks in Conroe, Texas. I was now amongst strangers who would care for me and see the most vulnerable sides of me. I was away from my husband and son, who were in Virginia. The one thing I did have was the comfort of knowing that my father-in-law and mother-in-law were with my daughter and that she was not alone. I was also very blessed with the fact that my sister-in-law came at a moment's notice to spend a few days with me and bring me all the necessities to make the hospital room more of a home.

Some asked why my husband was not there with me. I chose to not have him be there. I wanted him to focus on our son. There was nothing that could be done while I was in the first phase of recovery. I had moments of anger, fear, and blame. I had a wave of emotions because I could not understand why. *Why did this happen?*

I spent those next five weeks being absolutely pissed that I could not do simple movements that we take for granted. I could not get up by myself. I could barely sit up to eat because it hurt so freaking bad. I needed help, and I hated that I had to ask for it. The nurses became my new family. They saw me at my worst. They saw me cry angry tears. They saw me in my most vulnerable state, which was embarrassing and humbling at the same time. I had to learn how to walk again. In my mind, it was supposed to be simple. It was supposed to be like riding a bike again. I was supposed to just stand up and make it happen. It was not like that at all, and I was angry. With each surgery came new rules. I was to continue with physical therapy and occupational therapy, and I could only take showers with limitations. "No weight bearing on your left foot while you walk, take a shower, or go to the bathroom." *Are you kidding me?* I understood why I had these limitations, but I absolutely hated every second of it. Recovery was hard, and it hurt.

One of the things that helped me survive those weeks were string lights that my sister-in-law purchased from Target... the same ones that Haeli wanted. She brought those along with several other items that I could turn to when I didn't feel like eating hospital food or using hospital soap. These lights were battery-operated and in the shape of mini banners. They were not just any lights, though. These were now considered my very own party lights at the end of the tunnel. They were what I looked at each night as I lay alone in the hospital bed, crying myself to sleep. I knew that after all of the required surgeries were completed, I could go home. I needed to show improvement in my recovery and be self-sufficient enough to fly back home. Knowing this only made me work harder.

In the moment, I didn't realize how much support I received from friends and family. My high school friends came together to send my daughter and me comfort items and gift cards for when we were released. What some didn't know was that my daughter spent her eighteenth birthday in recovery with my in-laws at their house. It was far from what she had hoped for. But she was alive, and we were focusing on that.

I had so many people reach out, including my husband's chain of command, peers, and leadership, as well as my own little military family that I had met along the way. Some drove out to see me. They brought me meals, washed my hair, and braided it to make me feel human. If they are reading this, please know that I will forever be grateful to you for being there when I didn't know I needed it. From visits to care packages and phone calls, you saved me, and I will be forever grateful.

There were days where I was not able to physically get up to go to the bathroom without assistance. A portable toilet was placed next to my bed for those days where weight-bearing was not an option. There were days where I couldn't even wipe myself. Too much information? Yes, probably so. I tell you this because it was *hard*. This was real life. This is what I had to be humbled with in order to stop feeling sorry for myself. I had to work harder so that I could get the hell out of that hospital. I wanted to be back to what was going to be my new normal. I praise my physical and occupational therapists and the doctors and nurses that cared for me throughout those five long weeks. As each day passed, I grew a little bit physically stronger. Emotionally, I was a wreck. They were there when I cried and cursed out of frustration. I will forever be grateful to them for giving me my life back.

Why could I not just start walking as I did just weeks prior? Why did I now have all of these ugly scars all across the left side of my body? Why did this happen? *How did WE survive the accident?* No one knew, and that is all I kept hearing. I was tired of hearing it because I did not understand it myself.

After those five weeks, I was finally able to leave that Texas hospital and go home to Virginia. My sister-in-law and nephew flew me home because there was no way I could do it on my own. I required both a walker and a wheelchair. My entire left calf all the way down to my foot was in a boot that could only be taken off when I slept. This thing was keeping those plates and screws intact. Sounds crazy, right? And, you guessed it — no weight-bearing on it for at least three weeks. *Seriously?* But honestly, at that point, I didn't really care. I was cleared to go home, and that was all that mattered.

The plane ride home was painful. I kept losing feeling in my leg, but there was no way for me to elevate it. I wanted to scream and cry. Emotionally, I was not prepared for any of this, and my mental state was the last thing that I was taking care of. I pushed those feelings aside and went through the motions of just wanting to get home. I was also concerned that I would be putting more pressure on my family at home. They had enough to deal with, especially since Haeli had also flown back home to be with us, and my husband was going through military schooling. Haeli would stay until she was prepared for that second chance of starting her first college semester.

I sincerely want to thank my cousin, who drove in from Maryland just to pick us all up at the airport in Virginia. She was such a blessing when it came to relieving the stress of having my husband come get me. You must be thinking that my husband should have been there, but I made the decision to have him focus on

Haeli and Blaze. A part of me felt so much guilt for having all of these stressors put on him while he was attending military schooling.

When I arrived home, I continued my physical and occupational therapy. My neighbors were amazing — they offered me borrowed wheelchairs, shower seats, and so many other items I never thought I needed. Recovery was hell and a continued humbling experience. I was afraid of falling and terrified that I would break something again because that would add even more time to my recovery sentence. I felt like a burden when my kids had to wheel me around if I decided to leave the house. I also didn't want to go anywhere because I was not emotionally ready to be in a car again.

It took me six months after the accident to be able to drive again. I saw strength in my daughter whenever she offered to drive me around just to get out of the house. I often wondered how strong she really was because we both endured the same traumatic experience. How was she able to drive when I was absolutely terrified?

Throughout the next year, I had to constantly remind myself that I have been kept in this life for a reason. It was time for me to focus on how I was going to help myself so that I could help others. The self-healing journey was about to begin in full force, and I needed to be fully committed physically, mentally, and emotionally.

After some more hard lessons, tough love, and lots of pain, I learned that all of this happened *for* me and not *to* me. This realization made me wake up and open my eyes to what He had been planning for me. I hate my scars, but I love that I am alive to talk about them. I hate the pain, but I love the strength it has given me.

My mess is my message — a message of turning darkness to light. It is a process, but, in the end, there is always a message, even if we don't quite understand it yet.

3: ROLL CALL

Roll Call; the calling of a list of names, as of soldiers or students, for checking attendance.[5]

NOVEMBER 1984, SIMI VALLEY, CALIFORNIA

I WALKED INTO MY HOUSE right past my stepfather and went straight into my bedroom without saying so much as a "Hello" (to the best of my recollection). Sensing that something was wrong, my stepfather asked me if I was OK.

What happens next, and throughout the rest of this chapter, is both from my memories and from police reports that I was able to acquire from the Simi Valley Police Department.

Once my mom arrived home from work, I repeated to her what was mentioned to my stepfather. I had to explain to her that this sequence of events not only happened once but twice on two separate occasions. I didn't say anything the first time because what the man had told me caused me to live in fear. He led me to believe that he could get into a lot of trouble for what had taken place. I was so confused and felt so much guilt since he was the father of my childhood best friend. I felt like I had no other choice but to pretend as if it didn't happen.

The police arrived at my house and started asking me questions about what had occurred just hours prior. I was shaking, crying, and nervous as I did not know how I was going to explain that I was just molested by someone that my family had known and trusted. *Was this my fault? Was I going to get into trouble? How was I supposed to tell my best friend what her father had just done to me? How did I let this happen not once but twice?*

Hours seemed to go by from the time the police set foot in my house to when they finally left. Knowing that they were there to help didn't take away from how excruciating it was to answer their questions. I still couldn't process it all and was shaking while trying to explain the events to these strangers and my family, who were all staring at me. I was confused and even terrified that "he" was going to find out that it was me who reported him to the police. I did not know what he was capable of or if he would try and come after me. What no one knew was that he made me promise that I wasn't going to say anything because, if I did, he could go to jail.

I remember sitting in the front seat of the car and hearing him say, "Now, you have to promise that you are not going to say anything, alright?" I sat there with my heart practically beating right out of my chest and responded, "I promise." At nine years old, the only thing I could think of at that very moment was how to save myself from this man. While he made me promise that I wouldn't say anything, I crossed the fingers on my less visible right hand and all the toes on both of my feet so that he wouldn't see that I was lying. (This is what kids did back then. They would secretly cross their fingers, meaning they were hiding the truth, and that is exactly what I did.) I kept trying to get closer to the car door to see if, maybe, I could jump out somehow. As we drove up to each stoplight, I kept eyeing the door, hoping for a red light and trying to come up with an escape plan. I was just too afraid to open that door and jump out as I feared he would just come after me. The plan didn't go through. I stayed in the car and continued to let him drive me home.

What happened during the first event may be triggering for some. It is something I never could imagine happening to young girls. This man used tactics that caused me to feel guilty for even thinking of speaking up. So much so that I had tried to erase it from my mind.

I didn't want to upset him and get into any trouble as he was the one person my mom trusted to take us home from our after-school activities. I never imagined that my first kiss would be with an older man, old enough to be my own father. I was disgusted. I was shocked. I was scared. I was not able to get that image out of my head. How could someone do that to a little girl? I am filled with anger as I write this. I felt helpless and had no idea what would lie ahead of me.

Never did I imagine that any man would have had control over me to the point where I would keep everything a secret for so long. I would replay the moment over in my head, thinking if I had just jumped out of the car, it wouldn't have happened. If I would have just opened the car door. If I would have just pushed him away. But

I didn't. I couldn't. It wasn't that easy, but I still lived with that guilt for so many years. I never thought that he would state that I agreed to his advances. In the police records, he said that I asked to call him "Dad" and that I loved him. He also stated that I never said "no" to his advances.

———

How do you feel? Are you angry yet? Can you imagine what I was feeling while sitting in his car, just wanting to go home? How could any child agree to something like that?

I found out that I was not the only one who had been through a very similar series of traumatic events by him. Of those of us who reported what he had done to us, I was the only one willing to go to trial and testify in court. Now, I do not want to make it sound like I was the best and the bravest because no one can fathom what the parents or the children were going through. I just wanted something to be done, so I said I would do it. I didn't know what taking the stand would entail until later.

As a parent, I do not know how, or if, I would have ever kept calm in this situation. In fact, I may not even be here to tell this story from behind this computer. Writing this book may very well have been from a jail cell if anything like this had ever happened to one of my own children. Even though I have my own idea of how I would have handled these horrid events as a parent, I know that my parents did the best they could during this time.

"Are you sure you want to testify in court?" "Do you understand what the lawyers are going to ask you?" I remember nodding my head and saying, "I have to do this, or he will get away with it." I am not even sure how I had the strength to face this man in a courtroom full of strangers, including his lawyers defending him. No one can really prepare a child for what happens in the courtroom. To be asked questions that were purposely designed to confuse me was a distressing experience. "Is the man who did this to you in this courtroom?" "Can you point him out?" I was sick to my stomach as I raised my finger to point to him while having to look him in the face. It was absolutely terrifying. I did not want him to see me look in his direction. I wanted to hide and pretend that I wasn't there. I had to relive the moments of what he had done and literally try to convince these people that I was not lying. I was asked, "Are you sure that this is the man who did the things that you are saying?" I responded with a "Yes," almost with hesitation as they were skilled at trying to make a young girl second-guess herself.

I ended up changing schools as well as friends. That man went to jail, but for only nine months. I was shocked that it was for that short of time, and I was never sure why. I was just glad that he wasn't going to be around to do this again or for me to have to face him. To be honest, even though I was in a different school, it didn't change the fact that I still lived in fear. There were times where I thought I spotted him in a crowd. I could literally feel my chest tighten up and like I couldn't breathe when I thought I caught even a glimpse of someone that looked like him.

I was also very upset that I lost my best friend. I figured that she hated me and was angry at me for sending her dad to jail. I never spoke to her again, and it broke my heart. I can't imagine how she felt. I didn't even know how to contact her. As a matter of fact, while writing this, I did try to locate her on social media. But, I was not able to. That is as far as I went because part of me still feels the guilt, even though I know nothing was my fault.

The day I received the news that he was released from jail was almost as terrifying as when he went to jail. I got the call at my house. As I was listening to the person on the other line, my heart stopped. The only thing that could come out of my mouth was, "OK, so what do I do now?" I literally didn't know what I was supposed to do next. Was he going to try to find me? Would there be revenge? My mind was racing, and I didn't even want to leave the house.

"It is going to be OK" is what I heard on the other end of the phone. "He can't hurt you anymore." I took a deep breath and just prayed. I couldn't sleep for days. I had nightmares. I constantly looked over my shoulder. When was this going to end? How are you supposed to handle these types of situations? Nothing can prepare you. You end up being the type of person who just wants to forget anything ever happened. You learn how to mask the feelings, and you just suppress them for as long as you can… until you finally explode, as I did.

I always felt like he was watching me, even though the lawyers stated that he would never come after me again. It wasn't until I went to high school that I felt even remotely safe again. I felt that, now that I was older, I would be able to protect myself better. It was this incident that led my parents into placing my brother and me into Taekwondo classes. We practiced for ten years. It gave me the confidence I needed for the next several years of my life. I needed to feel that I could protect myself from someone, anyone, who might come after me again.

When I decided to include this part of my life in this book, I wanted to know what events took place so that I could gain the strength to keep moving forward with sharing this story, *my* story. I wanted to make sure that what I was stating was not just some kind of nightmare but the real truth of what shaped me into the person I am today. So, thirty-five years later, I contacted the Simi Valley Court and requested copies of the entire court files for my case. I anxiously waited for a response, not knowing how long it was going to take. This was during the time of COVID-19, and things weren't moving as quickly as they normally did. So, when they responded after just a few days, I was shocked. I wasn't even sure that they could locate the files, but, to my surprise, they did. And they were even willing to mail it all to me.

Waiting for the files to come in the mail felt like an eternity. I checked the mail as often as I could, sometimes a few times a day (probably bringing strange looks from our neighbors...). When the court case files finally came in the mail, everything stopped — my heart, my breath, my eyes that were now locked on this package, even time itself. I was shaking and nervous. It was like I was back in my nine-year-old body, feeling like his presence was still here. I questioned whether I was ready to read the transcript but decided to push through. It was time.

After reading over the police reports several times with the gruesome details of the events I had gone through, all of those ugly memories suddenly came back to me. This man literally placed his hands down my pants and over my "private" area. He actually stated that I never said that it was not OK. He really believed that nothing was wrong because I "didn't say no." I did push him away. I did try to stop him. But I was face to face with my best friend's father. What was I supposed to do? How could a nine-year-old have even comprehended all of this?

A hidden reason for why I wanted to read those court files was so I could get a clearer view of why I was so paranoid with my own children. I am not sure if it was the military side of me or my paranoia that made me question almost everything they did. Going to a friend's house was not an easy task. I had to meet the parents. I wanted to know what they did for a living. Who was going to be home, and for how long? The list could go on.

Talking about childhood sexual trauma was not a thing in the 80s. The news barely covered this type of story. But, as Haeli and Blaze grew up, there began to be more talk of sexual assaults on children as well as of kidnapping and sex trafficking. And with the internet growing how it did, it felt like I couldn't escape from hearing and reading about those stories. It was f'n ridiculous. How is someone not supposed to be paranoid all the damn time? I raised my children in fear and was overprotective. It took me years to learn to slowly let go. I raised my kids to be independent, yet I always had fear in the back of my mind.

The kids stated that I was too strict and that I didn't trust them. What they didn't realize was that it wasn't about them; it was about their friends' home environments and other people who could be there. You could say that it was difficult for me to trust people. I tried very hard to keep them safe, just as my mom tried to keep my brother and me safe. Never did she expect her daughter to face what I did — but how could anyone expect something like that? Although Haeli and Blaze know some of what happened to me as a child, they do not know the complete details, and I am not sure that I will ever be able to tell them.

I did go to counseling and had a very supportive family, but I still struggled with relationships. I struggled with trust and fear. I was afraid to date older men because I did not know what they would expect. I struggled with the fear of making people upset or not liking me. I struggled to gain acceptance.

I don't share this part of my life to gain pity or to put that broken-hearted feeling in you. I share this because I am now in a place where I can finally speak out about it. It is something that I could never freely open up about before. I needed to talk about it. I needed to acknowledge what happened so that I could free myself from the guilt, shame, and trauma. Having my own children forced me to start to see the world differently, and it was scary as hell. Haeli and Blaze are now twenty and eighteen. They have a good understanding of how the world works, and I can only hope, and I pray that I have prepared them for what is to come.

Childhood trauma has been an eye-opening experience. Although it consumed me for most of my life, I can say that, at the age of forty-five, being able to share this part of my life has been both freeing and terrifying. It is when we use our voice that we are more powerful. In fact, I will continue to use my voice by sharing the actual court files from my case. I have not decided if it will be on my website or in a new book, but sharing those files will enable us — *all of us* — to accurately process what needs to change in the court system and be better advocates for victimized children.

For those of you who are struggling with your own trauma, it will take time, and it won't be easy, but you will overcome. I believe that the first step is to acknowledge the space you're in. Understand that it was not your fault. Understand that you cannot let it define who you are. It happened to you, but it is not who you are.

I am done with letting my trauma make me feel like I was not worth anything better than a troubled relationship. I am done with it making me feel paralyzed. So, here is my story, and I am ready to be free.

4: FRAGO

FRAGO: *Fragmentary order. A fragmentary order is an abbreviated form of an operation order (OPORD), usually issued on a day-to-day basis, which eliminates the need for restating information contained in a basic operation order.*[6]

1988 – 1999, SIMI VALLEY, CALIFORNIA

I HAD JUST GRADUATED middle school and felt like such a big kid because I could now either walk or take the bus to school. This was the second school I attended during my elementary school days, and I stayed there straight into middle school. I had to leave the first school due to that one incident that changed the course of my life. It was at this second school that I found out that "he" was being released from jail. All I wanted to do was live a life where I didn't have to constantly look over my shoulder for fear that he would come to get me for what I had done.

I couldn't believe that I would be in junior high! I was already making plans for the next phase of my life. What I didn't know was that my mom had other plans for me. She was doing some research of her own and decided that an all-girl Catholic school would be a better idea. Are you thinking what I am thinking? Seriously! This was a crazy idea!

What some do not know was that I was quite a rebel in middle school. Some of you may be thinking, no way! Not Annette! ...Yeah, I was quite the character.

I may or may not have been caught behind the school building kissing a boy. I also may have had an eye-rolling problem in 5th grade, so much so that a parent-teacher conference was mandated… (I may be shrugging my shoulders right now). My mom thought I was a little boy-crazy and easily influenced and thought that I needed to be in a more controlled environment to prevent me from making those forbidden mistakes. To say that I was devastated was an understatement. I was pissed. I locked myself in the bathroom for over two hours after she broke the news to me. I hated how overprotective she was. She already knew who all of my friends were. Why was she trying to ruin my life?

Apparently, my mom was able to see part of my rebellious stage along with my attitude that was consuming my teenage years. She always told me that, even if she didn't see what I was doing in the present, it didn't mean that she wouldn't find out. Who would have known that I would be dealing with these same things with my own children? The "I hope your kids turn out just like you" curse was among us, and I was feeling it. "Thanks, Mom." It is funny how life changed for me and even more so after having my own daughter, who has her mother's same stubborn mindset. At this point of the story, I wish I could add all of the eye-rolling, wine glass, and dramatic face emojis.

I was never a girl who took school seriously. I always felt like I was just trying to stay afloat. I felt like I could be doing other things that were much more productive. I was the eye-roller, the talker, the sigher, and the take-it-day-by-day person. I was also the procrastinator and would commonly pull an all-nighter to study for a test. I was THE black sheep of the family. Can you relate?

Although my mom raised me to be financially independent personally and professionally, I still had sass, a stubborn head, and a voice that needed to be heard. I grew up shy, but as I got older, if you asked for my opinion, you would get it — and without a filter. It took many years for me to develop the courage to use my voice, state my opinion, or even raise my hand. I always tried to sit in the back because I didn't feel like I had enough to say that would make a difference.

I didn't always make the right decisions when it came to relationships. Because of the trauma I endured, I found comfort in conflicted boys who used verbal berating as a way to show that they cared about me. I also found myself surrounded by drama as a way to try to figure out my life and what was missing. At that time of my life, that lifestyle of having abusive relationships that were drenched with drama was how I coped with things that I had not yet dealt with.

Both my daughter and I are guilty of putting others' needs before our own. Instead of dealing with our internal struggles, we tend to find ourselves being inserted into unnecessary drama. We've also tried to fix self-inflicted drama that was, in fact, created by someone else. This behavior was a double-edged sword that often hurt everyone involved. It is not that I tried to find it intentionally — it was just a way to hide what I was really going through. Experiencing drama and trauma, as we have seen in the present, is not a gender-specific thing. Anyone can go through it. What my parents tried to do for me I wish I could have done for my own children. It is unfortunate when life has thrown us more bullets than our armor can protect us from. We continue to wear that protective helmet, but, sometimes, the enemy still gets us.

During the six years that I attended La Reina High School, the all-girls Catholic school, I realized that I wore a mask that no one could see. I wore different masks throughout each year. I was just trying to make it through high school, not knowing what my future was going to entail. Although the school worked tirelessly at preparing us for the outside world, I was just not one of those who were ready.

One of my friends enlisted in the Army right out of high school. In my mind, I thought, "Holy shit, 'V' joined the Army?" I was so intrigued that I actually had a recruiter come to the house, sit at my table, hand the papers to sign my life away... and then NOPE. I couldn't do it. I chickened out. I was scared. I wasn't ready for that type of commitment. Something told me to stay (for now...) and go to school.

I was always fascinated with the military. I did not know until later in life that my grandfather on my father's side was in the Peruvian Air Force, which I thought was one of the most fascinating things ever. I never did get to meet him as he passed away due to complications from a bullet wound when my dad was eleven. I also didn't know until years later that my uncle, my dad's brother-in-law, also served. He was in the US Army and served in one of the brigades that I also would serve in. I felt so honored to have been in the same space, even if it was decades later. Although I didn't grow up knowing my grandfather or even knowing that my uncle served, I still felt a strong connection to the military, and it helped to assure my reasons for joining.

After that embarrassing incident with the recruiter and my fear of something that many of our young soldiers do every day, I decided to attend community college before making any rash decisions. I completed my associate degree in a year and a half at Moorpark Community College, met a boy named Robert, and moved to Arizona to attend Arizona State University (ASU) to be closer to him.

Now, before you go and roll your eyes and think to yourself, "Why did she do that?" let me explain. Robert was from an amazing family with whom I felt a strong connection. Something told me to take this chance, go for it, and not to let anything stop me. We met while we were working at a local retail store. He was younger than me but very mature for his age. We got along very well and felt a strong bond. When the news came that his family was moving to Arizona, I made the decision that I would try and follow. When choosing a university, one of the requirements for me was that the university had to have a program to train for the

Army, a psychology department, financial aid, and a physical location. I applied to only two schools. I didn't have the best grades, and I could no longer be financially dependent on my parents.

————

WHAT CAME NEXT WILL be a surprise to you as it was for me.

I was accepted into ASU and the Reserve Officers' Training Corps (ROTC) program. Robert and I broke up about six months later. Yes, I was devastated. Yes, I was pissed. After shedding many tears, I decided that I could not go back home. I had to prove to myself that I could do this. I decided to take the leap and make that move to Arizona. Robert decided that he needed to see other people his age. After months of heartbreak and trying to figure out my life, I realized what I needed to do next.

I knew that my mom was not going to be able to financially support me on this next journey in my life. I applied to ASU knowing that I would have to apply for the financial assistance offered and that it would be at the out-of-state residency cost. It was brutal. I moved several times, worked several different jobs, and fought my way into becoming an Arizona resident just to cut down on costs. It took me two years to finally be accepted as an Arizona resident, which included meeting with the University's financial assistance board. I literally cried when they finally accepted me.

Many may be asking why I didn't use the ROTC scholarship. Remember when I mentioned that I didn't take school seriously? My lack of taking things seriously affected my grades, and it followed me. I was therefore not eligible for free money. It took five years and $35 thousand of student debt to grow the hell up.

Even with all the stress of college life, military training, and boys, I look back to those days as an experience that will never be forgotten. My brother and our childhood friend got accepted into ASU, and we all attended college together for our last two years there. They saw me make mistakes, yet they provided sound advice when it was needed. I may have been the oldest, but I was not always the smartest. I experimented with some college drinking and recreational activities, yet I survived somehow. I really have to thank the ruthless, early-morning, ass-kicking military training that I willingly participated in every single day, and I don't regret any of it. I did not join a sorority because of all the rules, yet I joined the Army with the most rules. I never stated that my life choices made sense, but it may very well have made me into the strongest person I could have been.

I moved into two different dorms, an apartment, a townhome, and Robert's parents' place during my college days. Do you want to know something funny about these moves? How in the world did I end up moving in with Robert's parents after we broke up? Well, before and after the breakup, I formed a really great relationship with his family. His family took me in as their own and helped me gain stability both educationally but emotionally as well. What they did for me was much more than I could have ever asked for. I think one of the most difficult things that really helped me move past things was attending Robert's wedding. Over the years, we have remained in contact, and it has been such a blessing to see how their family has grown. Twenty-five years later, Robert and I are still friends, and I'm still very close to his family and siblings. They all have beautiful families of their own.

What was the point of all of this? To say that, sometimes, those crazy decisions turn into good ones. I never thought that I would have moved for a boy, much less stayed and faced what I thought was one of the most difficult times in my life... and that was just the beginning.

Just when I had sworn off dating, trying to stay focused on finishing college, I met my husband. The funny thing is that I met him during military training, and I thought he was the biggest jerk that I ever had to deal with. He was already commissioned and was one of the training instructors for us cadets. He was tough and gave no slack. If he saw you, you were to render the proper salute as he was an officer, and we were officers in training.

During training, he was a hardass. I really could not stand him. We did training involving the high dive at ASU's pool. I was already afraid of heights, so doing this was making me uneasy. It involved us being in full uniform, having a dummy rifle, and being blindfolded. As I hit the edge of the diving board and was getting ready to jump, I hesitated. I was already trying to gain the courage to jump, so I was freaking out a little bit. He didn't show any remorse. He said, "What are you doing, cadet?" while he grabbed my arm and pushed me over that already-terrifying high dive. That just added more fuel to the fire. I was convinced I hated this guy.

For some reason, a year after the first time that I met him, we ran into each other in the cadet lounge. That lounge was for all of us who were going through the ROTC training. The last thing I expected was to agree to go on a date with him, let alone marry him. We got married in September of 1998.

Shortly after getting married, I was given an opportunity to attend either Airborne School at Fort Benning, GA, or a three-week training in Vincenza, Italy. Although Airborne School sounded like an amazing opportunity, and it was not afforded to many, I chose to go to Italy. I mean, who wouldn't? I had never left the United States, so I jumped at the chance to go. See what I did there?

As soon as I arrived on-ground, I found out that I was training with an airborne unit (go figure) and that the unit was NOT conducting their training in Italy but in Germany. If any of you are nodding your head because you can guess where in Germany, then keep reading. It was, indeed, not one of the most visited towns by tourists but by the military. If you guessed that this luxurious place was Grafenwöhr, then you are correct! There was nothing there except large amounts of land, which were perfect for training. The funny thing was that back in those days, the German pubs in the training areas were still open, and you were allowed a two-beer minimum. On the off days or even after training, we would venture to the pub to have beer and bratwurst. I will always cherish that part of Grafenwöhr and the camaraderie that our unit had.

During this training, I was just the cadet who wore the beret with the rank of a circle, also known as the dot. It is what set us newbies apart, and we were often made fun of for it. I was a little naive and clearly new to being around a whole unit of predominantly male soldiers, which definitely made me stand out. And my shy demeanor didn't help. I was there to shadow a first lieutenant and learn the skills of being a leader. I wanted to learn how to be strong and be taken seriously, especially as a female. I put on my game face and went through the motions. We still had about four days left in Italy before heading off to Germany. The city of Vicenza was amazing. I was invited by a few of the soldiers to tour some of the sites before departing. I trusted them as I didn't have any reason not to.

―――――――

Or so I thought.

During those last few days in Italy, I agreed to do some sightseeing with a fellow soldier. Little did I know that he would take advantage of my unfamiliarity with the military culture. I had no reason not to trust a person in uniform, let alone a soldier. His advances towards me shook me to the core. I was speechless. I was shaken. I didn't know what to do. So, I went with the unit to Germany for their training exercise and suppressed what had happened. I just acted as nothing happened, yet it was tearing me up inside.

I did not want to be seen as the weak female who was new to the whole Army thing. I didn't want to stay behind and miss out on an opportunity. Taking part in this training was the whole reason why the Army sent me here. I kept quiet until I was no longer able to act as if nothing happened. I decided to tell the same lieutenant whom I had been shadowing. I don't remember if I told him all the details, but it was enough for him to help me leave halfway through that three-week training so that I could be away from that soldier. I didn't give any names. I was afraid to point out the one who had just scarred my first real experience in a training environment. I just wanted to go back home to my new husband, graduate from ASU, get my commission, and forget that any of this ever happened.

As I prepared to go back to the states, I learned that one of my former senior leaders from college was here. He had just moved to Germany and was working on the same installation that I was on. I didn't know who else I could confide in, so I went to him. I still get angry to this day when I share this part of the story. That senior leader took advantage of me and the situation to the point that left me questioning if I could ever trust anyone else. I was so angry. I was hurt. I was shocked. *How could he do this to me?* I trusted him. I left feeling paralyzed. I went back to my training area and waited to get the hell out of there.

I got back home to Arizona, reported that senior leader, and didn't push the issue because I was scared. That senior leader was someone who helped train us. He was someone that we trusted. So, I didn't think anyone would believe me. I thought that they would say I imagined it or made it more dramatic than it really was. If you are reading this and getting angry because "I should have done this," or "I should have done that," please keep some things in mind. This was the late-90s where this type of thing was not spoken of. We kept conversations like this to ourselves. I just lived with it, put on my game face, and moved on. That may not have been the healthiest reaction, but it was all I knew how to do. I did not report that first incident that happened with the other soldier. Those experiences affected the way I saw my male counterparts. A part of me was skeptical. I wasn't sure how to view them. I was almost afraid. It made me nervous about being around them.

Over time, my game face turned into a bitch face. When I was a cadet, I got told that I smiled too much. I wasn't sure how to take that and was surprised that it was a problem. *So, you are telling me that I need to change who I am in order to be successful in the Army? WTF?* Nonetheless, I was driven to succeed in that mostly male (and apparently non-smiling) environment. So, I tried to wipe that smile off of my face in order to train myself to be a hard charger. That only lasted for so long. That wasn't who I was. Smiling was my way of pushing past the most difficult of times. I even cried when I was really pissed. It was inevitable that I wore my heart on my sleeve and my emotions on my face. I was an empath, and nothing was going to take that away from me. I tried so hard to be the "tough guy." Over the years, I was just a volcano waiting to erupt. I never stopped smiling. I cared too much, and when you got me upset, it was already past the point of crossing the line. I ended up becoming very bitchy. I cared for my soldiers deeply, but if you pissed me off, I was going to call you on it. I never used to be that way. I used to be the shy person who wouldn't know how to confront you and didn't want to cause any problems.

To say that the military changed me is an understatement. The good thing is that I ended up figuring out who I was, standing up for what I believed in, and fighting for a fair chance. I can say that I am a stronger person now and have found my voice. I chose not to let my trauma consume me anymore. I chose to use my mess as my message in order to help others. I chose to live instead of suffering.

Once you are able to acknowledge that you are not what happened to you, you can begin the self-healing process. I am here to help you begin.

5: SANDBOX

The term sandbox usually refers to Iraq, sometimes Kuwait. Secret Squirrel: Highly classified, top secret. Secrecy confers tremendous status upon soldiers; the most classified missions are often the most prestigious in soldiers' eyes.[7]

2000 – 2003, HANAU, GERMANY

2004 – 2005, FORT LEONARD WOOD, MISSOURI

2005 – 2006, IRAQ (OEF 05/06)

2004 – 2010, FORT HOOD, TEXAS

I SPENT SIX YEARS stationed at Fort Hood, Texas. This was not the norm for military life. A normal length of time at a duty station is typically between one and three years long, depending on location and whether it is stateside or overseas. We expected to stay at Fort Hood for three years. We ended up staying longer because my husband applied for a master's program at Baylor University and was accepted. This also came with a price. He incurred more time both in service and at our current location.

During those six years at Fort Hood, many changes happened. Although certain parts of the story will remain private, I will tell you that I started losing sight of the person I was becoming. I was afforded opportunities that I never thought I would have had. I was also surrounded by leaders, soldiers, and peers who taught me many lessons on how to survive the culture. I was practically raised in the Field

Artillery culture as well as the Light and Heavy Infantry cultures. The people I was surrounded by were what I considered badasses. They were hungry for knowledge and experiences, and I was hungry to be part of it. Although that was not my first duty station, there was something about that place that forever changed me.

My first official duty station prior to Fort Hood was in Hanau, Germany. Although I had been there before for training, Germany was the first place I had officially lived in outside of the United States. I was twenty-three years old and four months pregnant with Haeli — nervous and excited at the same time. How the hell was I going to figure out my life as a soldier, mother, *and* military spouse? All at the age of twenty-three. I look at my twenty-year-old daughter now and can't believe the things that I experienced at her age. There was no book to tell you how to navigate this part of my life. Especially while in the Army. I didn't really have anyone to ask advice from. I kind of just went with it and prayed for some wisdom along the way.

When I arrived in Germany, my husband was in the field. I was assigned a sponsor to shadow who was a first lieutenant. They were to show me what to expect as a soldier and how to live in a new country. I lived out of a *gasthaus* (German hotel) for a little over a month. I was on an emotional rollercoaster as I was feeling alone and really missing my family. *What am I doing, and how did I get here?* This was my first time as a real soldier at my first duty station in a different country, and there was no turning back.

I was assigned to the 16th Corps Support Group in Hanau, Germany, located at Hutier Kaserne (*kaserne* is German for barracks). It was a small base with a few other units. It was our own little community where we knew just about everyone. Little did I know that it would also be the community that we would be protecting. This is where I was when 9/11 happened. I was sitting at my desk when I heard what had taken place — just a day before, four planes crashed into the Pentagon and the Twin Towers. Since we were nine hours ahead, we didn't receive the information until after it all happened.

As soon as the information was passed down, all kasernen were on lockdown, and some of us quickly became part of the quick reaction force teams. I quickly became part of a team that would be pulling guard duty to be on watch in increments of 24-hour shifts. This was not something I ever envisioned doing within the first two years of being in the Army. At this point, our awareness was heightened, and we were fully aware of how serious this was. This was no longer a practice exercise. This was the real thing.

My husband and I were not stationed on the same kaserne. The US military was spread throughout Germany on several different kasernen. Because of our varying locations, we decided to split the difference and lived amongst the German community (also known as living on the economy). We lived in a quaint neighborhood in the town of Limeshain-Himbach. German living was a unique lifestyle, yet it was something that we grew to love. We lived in a third-floor flat with very high ceilings, tiny windows, and no closets. Even through my broken German, we adapted very well and made some long-lasting friendships. Some of those friendships have even lasted over twenty years since we left. Thank you to the people who cared for my children as if they were their own. Your presence in our lives will forever be cherished.

Three years and two children later, my husband received orders for a permanent change of station (PCS) back to the states. This happened quickly and prevented me from joining my unit on their deployment to Afghanistan. I felt very guilty for not going with them, but I had to choose my family. I received my orders to travel back to the US with my husband and PCS to Fort Leonard Wood, Missouri, where we attended the Captains Career Course and completed our master's degrees with our three-year-old daughter and one-year-old son.

During our ten-month training at Fort Leonard Wood, we both had to really learn how to adapt and overcome. We were both constantly tested as parents and students. We had to schedule times to use our one computer so we could get our school assignments done. We had to take turns parenting our young children. We had to learn how to deal with different stressors than we had in Germany. There were many arguments and sleepless nights. I was not sure how I was going to make it.

Training could not stop just because we had our family there. It didn't matter if both parents were soldiers. We had to figure out a way, even if it took several family care providers and daycare centers. Waking up your children at 0430 to drop them off at a stranger's house was never an easy task. We had to be at formation by 0530, and it was up to us to figure out what to do with our kids. It was a stressor I never truly comprehended until then. I did not know how I was going to do this parenting and soldiering thing. Attending training with children while attempting to work towards a master's degree was a lot different than being in a training environment.

This dual-military lifestyle was not easy. It sucked. It was hard, and I felt overwhelmed and exhausted. I was trying to juggle so many things. All I wanted to do was make it through my military training. Then, the unexpected happened. Sometime during the summer of 2004, I suffered from gallbladder pancreatitis and had to have emergency surgery. The surgery put me out of training long enough to delay the process of completion and graduation. I was recycled into another class and graduated later than my husband. He was forced to move to our next duty station at Fort Hood, Texas, due to an upcoming deployment. I was left with both kids while he prepared for his next duty assignment. How about that for family life?

Some do not realize what goes on behind the scenes of a dual-military family. My brother flew to Missouri to help me take the three-day trek to Texas. By the time the kids and I arrived, my husband was already gone. He had purchased a house for us, set up our beds and a small number of toys for the kids, and left. I remember crying on the drive through Texas. It felt like the longest three days, and I just wanted to get to our new home. We survived the treacherous drive, but it sucked.

November 2005, it was my turn to deploy. At this time, my brother-in-law was stationed at Fort Hood with us. My father-in-law moved to Texas and purchased a house a few blocks down the street. My mother also ended up moving from California. She purchased a house and prepared to help with the kids while I was deployed. Little did we know that my husband, my brother-in-law, and I were going to be gone at the same time.

My brother-in-law deployed first, I deployed second, and my husband followed six months after. I was given an amazing opportunity to take command of a new company of soldiers that was heading to Iraq under the 4th Infantry Division. As a chemical officer, this was a rare offer. So when I was presented with the position, I held back the tears and graciously accepted it.

My husband and I were company commanders at the same time. I knew that it was one of his dreams but never realized how much it was also one of mine. We did not expect to be in similar roles and deploy within months of each other, so we had to react quickly.

I packed and repacked my duffle bags more times than I could count. I had not deployed before, so I didn't know what to bring with me. Yes, we did have a packing list, but for some reason, I wanted to pack my full-sized shampoo bottles and all the things that I was so used to having (insert face-palm). No, people, you should not do that!

The location we were going to had shoppettes to buy the essentials, and we were able to receive mail. Anything that I could not fit into my bags, I was able to have shipped to me. I left in the middle of the night without saying goodbye to my kids. They were three and five, and we felt it was best to leave them in the way we did — tucked in bed. They knew that I was leaving. They knew that I had to "protect the soldiers."

I didn't want them to have the memory of dropping me off on base in the dark. My husband drove me to the parking lot where I would meet my soldiers, who became my main focus during this deployment. It was now my job to be with them on our way there and back. I needed to bring them home safely. I saw their mothers and fathers days prior, knowing that I was responsible for their child. It was overwhelming, exciting, and stressful. I was so grateful for this opportunity, but I was also worried about my children back home. *Would my husband and mom be able to handle all the things that I took care of? Would the kids be OK without me?* I couldn't even think about all the things that I would be missing, and it broke my heart. But I needed to get my head in the game if we were going to survive this deployment.

We left the parking lot and went into the holding area where we would wait to take the plane to an unfamiliar place in a whole different country. The process was long and emotional. We would sit in a large room with only chairs, some snacks, and tables. For those of us who were tired, we would lay our duffle bag on the ground and use our rolled-up jacket as a pillow. With our phones plugged into the walls, we would spend as much time as we could talking to our loved ones until it was time to go. Our first stop, Kuwait.

Exhausted and nervous, we arrived in the desert. It was hot. It was dusty. It was not pleasant. But we knew there was no way out of this one. We were here, and it was very real. Our stomachs in knots, we looked around at the base camp and tried to take it all in. This is where we would spend the next few weeks preparing for our final destination. We slept in large tents separated by gender.

Our days were now mundane and seemed like they would never end. Because our focus shifted to doing what we were trained to do, the days all just ran together. We didn't have set hours or weekends off. We did the training until it was complete and correct. Our uniform now consisted of our battle dress uniform and a weapon. Our family was now each other. We would call home when we could, not when we felt like it. We always wanted to call home, but we needed to remain focused. We had to learn how to change our mindset and, for some of us, that was not an easy task. Being here was still a surreal experience. A few weeks later, we were preparing for our next trip.

———

Final destination, Iraq.

We had arrived. After the flight and a very long bus ride, we arrived at the place where we would call home for the next twelve months. We got off the bus, took a deep breath, wiped our sleepy eyes, and looked around at the forward operating base (FOB) we would be housed in. We unloaded our duffle bags, grabbed what was ours, and walked to our new homes. In each trailer, we had a bed and a locker. It was such a lonely and strange feeling to walk into a room that didn't have the things that we were used to. We were now staring at empty walls and floors and the duffle bag that we came with. Each day after that, we started to get used to the fact that we only had each other for the next year. It was up to us to keep up the morale and stay focused on the mission — and I made a promise to myself that I would try and do that for all of us.

The headquarters was run by the commander, who was a commissioned officer, and the first sergeant, who was a non-commissioned officer. We were the team along with the soldiers that held the family together. Due to our mission, our soldiers were trained in a variety of tasks, one of them being to conduct convoys. Each convoy was always an unnerving experience. When I was not able to go on the convoys, I would be behind the scenes in the tactical operations center (TOC), keeping track of their movements. The convoys that I was able to go on sparked a certain level of awareness that I had never experienced before. I want to say that we were in the safe zone, but we could never let our guard down and had to be prepared for anything. We were still pretty much scared shitless. A convoy could take an hour to several, and even if we were tired, we were too scared to fall asleep. We had to make sure to keep the driver awake and keep an eye on our surroundings.

That year took a toll on us emotionally, and we were tired of being tired. We missed our families. We missed home. Each day seemed like Groundhog Day, and there was no escape. It was freaking hard. One of the little things that we looked forward to was the menu at the chow hall, also known as the dining facility (DFAC). We were co-located with several other small FOBs, and each one had its own DFAC that served different meals on each day of the week. One of our favorites was soul food with collard greens, catfish, and mac and cheese, or surf n' turf, which consisted of fried shrimp or even lobster tails. At this point, eating a good meal would sometimes be the highlight of our day.

One of my favorite memories was when my sister-in-law would send me care packages filled with all the girlie stuff. I was able to give myself my own manicure and pedicure. Trust me when I say that it was pure excitement to be able to do that. I specifically remember having a small, plastic kids swimming pool. If I remember correctly, we were able to purchase those at our local shoppette. This was used on those occasions where our water was shut off, and we had to bathe with water bottles in that small little kiddie pool. You might be thinking, "Hell no!" Oh yes, it happened. We had to do what was necessary. Now, we all did not use this pool idea. We did have access to our trailer showers and water bottles, but for some of us, we used the kiddie pool option. It was certainly a learning experience and something I learned to appreciate quickly. At least we had water, right? Throughout the rest of the deployment, we truly learned that family was not just about blood. It was more than that. We never realized how much that closeness was going to play into our lives, not until later.

I want to make note that this was not a terrible deployment. Things could have been much worse, but being deployed had its own stressors. There are several reasons why we come back the way we do. It does not always necessarily have to do with whether we were in combat or not. We do not always need to be in direct fire. Deployments come with their own scenarios that can change a person, and we didn't know how to talk about it. Oftentimes, we do not know how to share those invisible wounds, not even with our closest friends. We feel alone, ashamed, and confused. We do not know how to talk about our feelings because we spend too much trying to be tough. The fear of letting my emotions show led to masking it in anger and very little (if any) patience at all.

Any little thing set me off, and I was convinced that no one would understand. I was also not in the mood to be judged. I was a female officer wanting to progress in this career, and I didn't want anything to be held against me. I did not know how to communicate these feelings, not even to my husband. Instead, I just became more and more of a bitch. I had mood swings that made me incapable of saying how I felt. It was easier for me to just lash out.

Because my husband and I process our feelings differently, I had no idea that he was experiencing conflicting emotions from the same deployment time frame as me due to incidents that had happened. I learned that just because we processed them differently didn't mean that he was not going through something. It was me who didn't know how to communicate effectively. I am already a stubborn and hard-headed individual, so to ask for help or show any signs of weakness was not going to happen. I was convinced that I could take care of whatever it was that I was going through on my own. Clearly, that was not the case.

If you are reading this and nodding your head, you are already feeling this, aren't you? Does this sound all too familiar? My question to you is, What are you going to do about it? Please don't tell me that you are thinking, "I've got this." I said those same words for far too long. I wish I would have known that it was OK not to be OK. I wish I would have listened to that inner voice that was saying this was not the best way of dealing with my shit. I was spiraling and didn't realize how far I was going.

My hope is to help you find your voice so that you can share your story, process these emotions, and share your feelings without the fear of judgment or feeling ashamed or confused. My hope is that you will reach out and ask for help. I want you to know that you can still be a badass, all while seeking the help that is needed. I wish I would have reached out sooner and had the support. I had to stop thinking "if only." The time is now, and you can do this. I know how it felt to keep a close and tight hold of how I was truly feeling.

I want you to know that you are not alone and that I am here for you.

6: R&R

> R&R, military slang for rest and recuperation (or rest and relaxation or rest and recreation or rest and rehabilitation), is an acronym used for the free time of a soldier or international UN staff serving in unaccompanied (no family) duty stations.[8]

2006, FORT HOOD, TEXAS

DURING OUR TIME IN IRAQ AND BECAUSE OF THE LENGTH of the deployment, we were afforded the opportunity of taking R&R leave, which was at least two weeks. I chose to take the two weeks to come back home because I needed to see my kids. Sometimes, the phone calls and the video conferencing just were not enough. I wanted to see my kids in person.

Coming back home changed me, even though it was for a short amount of time. I didn't know what to do with all of these feelings and mixed emotions. Although I was relieved to be home, I was also very stressed. I now had to deal with things that I didn't really have to worry about over the past six months.

Once the unit redeployed back to our homes in the US for R&R, we went through a reintegration process that consisted of going through classes and briefings that were meant to prepare us for life back home. One of the things I wish I could have changed was I lied to myself and on the piece of paper that asked if we had any thoughts or feelings of depression. I paused for a moment when staring at that question. I questioned what would happen if I stated the truth. *What would people think? Who would find out?* I was not willing to risk it, so I rushed to fill out the paperwork. I later found out that I was not the only one with similar feelings.

After helping to take care of the kids while we were deployed, my mom undoubtedly needed a break from my four- and six-year-olds. She didn't realize that falling back into the routine was going to take some time for me. I couldn't just jump back into "normal" life as soon as she thought I could. I started to display many mixed emotions. It started with anger, then road rage. I had little to no patience with the smallest of things. The stressors of being back home were completely different than the stressors of being in Iraq, and I didn't know how to deal with them. I was trained for battle, not for this. I learned how to mask my true feelings, and I continued to suppress them for years.

———

I WISH I WOULD HAVE KNOWN how to communicate what was going on inside of me.

I wish I would have known that it was OK to not be OK.

I wish I would have known I was not alone.

I was a leader. I was in charge of soldiers. How would it look if there was something "wrong" with me? The thing is, there was nothing wrong with me. I was just dealing with so many mixed emotions that I couldn't see clearly. I kept thinking that I would be treated or looked at differently. In order to be competitive in obtaining other leadership roles, there was no way that I could let these emotions consume me. I worked too hard at gaining my secret clearance, and I sure as hell wasn't going to lose it over this.

Although it was good to be back home, part of me couldn't wait to get back downrange. I was anxious and anticipating the inevitable. I was going to have to go back to Iraq. My mindset was already programmed for it, making it difficult to just enjoy the time I had in the present with my family. It was as though I was trying not to get comfortable being home because I knew that I was going to have to go back. I spent a lot of time outside of the house shopping for things that I didn't really need. I started to become really good at emotional retail therapy. Buying things to make me happy in the moment to mask the deeper feelings. I didn't know how to just sit still. It was such a vicious cycle of emotions that I didn't know how to take control of.

There are times where soldiers do not take advantage of their R&R leave. Those who had deployed before knew and understood how difficult it could be to come home for a short amount of time while knowing that they will have to leave again. It was almost better to just not come home.

Since that was my first time being away from the kids and on a deployment, I had no idea what was in store for me. I didn't realize how happy and sad I could be at the same time. Instead of being happy with the fact that I was at home with my kids, I was on edge and counting the days that I had left with them. It was depressing. I could barely sleep. I could barely focus. I was a mess, but I never realized how much of a mess I truly was until years later.

Downrange, we had opportunities to take part in video teleconference calls (VTC), which is like Zoom. Each month, there was a schedule of available times where we could sign up for certain time slots. Due to the lack of available times and frequent technical issues, it did not always happen. I remember getting up in the middle of the night, around 2 a.m., to go talk to the kids. It was emotional but important for them to be able to see me. I was very grateful to have had that opportunity given to us. We also used VTC to communicate with our Family Readiness Groups and soldiers back home on rear detachment who were all helping to take care of our families. It was important for us to use every means available to keep the communication and morale of all involved during this deployment.

I look back at how I started spiraling emotionally due to the changes of being in Iraq and then coming back home. I didn't know how to process those feelings. I felt like I was climbing this mountain, not knowing where it was going to lead. The elevation kept rising, and I was losing air. I felt empty.

Most of the soldiers took R&R leave at different times so that we could always have part of the company continuing the mission. We could not stop focusing on what we were trained to do. For those of us who had never deployed before, this was a difficult task.

When I deployed to Afghanistan a few years later during the spring of 2008, I thought that coming back home for R&R would have been a little bit easier, but it was worse than when I came back from Iraq. The deployment location and mission were different. I thought that I would be more prepared, but I felt like I really lost control. This time, I came back home with more rage. I was more distant and lost, and I didn't know how to release what was going on inside of me. I was a volcano just waiting to erupt. In my mind, I became really good at hiding my invisible wounds. I kept doing what I knew how to do best, and that was to be a soldier.

My way of coping did not involve the art of communication. I did not know how to say what was wrong. I wore so many hats that I often couldn't distinguish which one I had on. I felt the pressure of having to be strong. It felt like I was a tiny boat in a massive ocean, just waiting for that next wave to hit. I could only do so much, but I felt I had to prove something bigger. I kept doing what I knew how to do best. I bottled up all of those emotions and kept wearing the same mask, all while switching out hats for every role that needed to be played. It is almost like the feelings I had every time we would move to a different duty assignment. With each move came more stress. You want to get settled in and unpack those boxes, but in the back of your mind, you know that you will have to pack them again for the next move in another year or two or three. I have never really been able to feel settled. I kept most of those boxes packed because I didn't want to stress over packing them again. I unpacked the necessities but also did some retail therapy to mask that stress. I tried to replace it with pretty things to make the house feel like a temporary home. This may or may not make sense to you, but I didn't know any other way to deal with all of the changes.

The military lifestyle changed me in so many ways. I lost patience. I lost my voice. I became really good at "pretending" and playing role games. There are so many games that this can be compared to, but the only one I was playing against was me. I was my worst critic, enemy, and opponent. If you have watched the Netflix series *The Queen's Gambit*, this may make more sense to you. My life seemed like a never-ending game of chess, hence why I was always my own worst opponent. I never knew when to make the right move and let my emotions take control of me. Rather than sit and ponder on where to move on the chessboard, I went for the quick and easy draw to wipe out what was right in front of me. I kept staring at the pieces and the players without regard to what their next move could be. I was a glutton for punishment. I didn't realize that all these waves of emotions from being lost would be heard loud and clear with the word "checkmate." My own life just kicked my ass.

But, in the end, I became really good at finding my voice, playing those roles, and using that critical side of me only to become better. It only took me another thirteen years to get here, but I am now able to breathe again. I still have a "don't F with me" side and a witty composition, but I am able to recognize when I am about to be in full-on bitch mode and say something out of turn.

Because of COVID-19 and the stay-at-home order, I feel a little more settled in at home. I am able to just live with what is around me and appreciate more of the things that I have taken for granted. If I were still serving and had to go through this again, I would be better equipped emotionally to handle the hard stuff. I would probably have a better handle at which chess pieces to move and where. I was getting a better handle on this life.

The struggle is real, but you are much stronger than you think. We are always going to be put in some real hard and shitty situations, but how we handle them is what matters. I have learned that this applies to just about every damn thing.

What I did next is going to probably shock the shit out of you. Keep reading to the next chapter.

7: BACK TO THE SANDBOX

Back to the Sandbox — not back to the fun place you take your kids go to build sandcastles. For military personnel, it's a term used to describe a forward-deployed position that is located in a desert.[9]

2007 – 2009, FORT HOOD, TEXAS

I WAS ASSIGNED TO THE 3rd Brigade, 1st Infantry Division as the brigade chemical officer. Our unit was set to deploy, and I was a part of the rear detachment. The roles and responsibilities of the rear detachment staff are nothing to take lightly. I never truly understood or appreciated what they did behind the scenes. Just because one does not deploy does not mean that they are contributing any less than those who deployed. Some of the responsibilities consisted of maintaining a strong Family Readiness Group (FRG). For those who aren't familiar, the FRG is an essential part of the command team and is made up of family members, volunteers, and soldiers belonging to a unit. They provide support, assistance, and resources when needed. We had a great team of FRG leaders, and it showed — especially when we needed them the most.

We had some of the best hard-working soldiers on our rear detachment team. We all worked tirelessly to do what was needed. I will never forget our small team that was in constant communication via email and phone. One of our funniest memories was when there were three of us females who all had names that started with the letter A, and our boss would constantly get confused about who was who. Because of that, we ended up trying to keep updated on each other's tasks so that we could keep him informed. Although we were not deployed, working from behind the scenes certainly had its trying moments.

We also had volunteers who were trained to be casualty assistance officers (CAO) and/or casualty notifications officers (CNO). For me, these were the most difficult roles to play. I volunteered to be trained as both because part of me felt like I needed to do more since I was not deploying with the unit. I felt a sense of guilt, and it consumed me enough to volunteer to go forward.

During my time in the rear, I felt so many mixed emotions. I knew that training for California and CNO was important, but I guess I never really knew what to expect. For those of you who really know me, you know how emotional I am. I am a huge softy and care deeply for people. I feel such deep feelings that it can sometimes be a bad thing, which is something that was hard for me to admit.

When we had a casualty downrange, it hit me. *Hard.* When I had to make that notification to the family, it hit me even harder. Just to make note, we are fully trained and have a binder full of information to prepare us for the most difficult of tasks. We also have a chaplain on standby who travels with us. The first notification I had to make caused me to sit in the car afterward and cry hard and long tears. It took everything for me to not break down with the family. It was almost like a scene in the movies. We show up in our uniforms then knock on the door and greet them with basically no emotion on our faces. We had to be the strong ones, and it ate at me. The spouse screamed and fell to the floor. We entered the house and made sure that there was family that could come to be with them before we left. Even writing this is bringing chills all across my body. I remember this as if it happened yesterday. I will never forget that moment.

My next mission was as the CAO. When a family loses a loved one, the CAO helps the family navigate through the process of what to do next. The families are so full of emotions that it is nearly impossible to think straight. I was there to assist a military spouse whose spouse had passed away from a heart attack while deployed at the young age of 38. As the CAO for this military spouse, I also served as someone she could contact to ask questions or even just provide a listening ear to when needed. I couldn't imagine how she was feeling about what life was going to be like next. This process was so heart-wrenching, and it was something that I did not take lightly. It made me see life in a whole different light. Oftentimes when we think we are prepared, we realize how much we did not have those much-needed and hard discussions.

This all took a toll on me emotionally. Although what I was doing in the background as part of the rear detachment was crucial, I still felt like I wanted and needed to do more. I asked to be sent forward with the rest of our unit. I wanted to deploy to Afghanistan. Was that a crazy move? Probably. Did it hinder my family? Absolutely. I didn't fully comprehend that I was probably not in the right mindset to be sent overseas for a second time. In my mind, I was already full of emotions and still didn't fully process them in the correct way. Unfortunately, this is a common trend. Many of us just do what we are told. For me, I was exhausted but didn't want to admit it.

My commander gave me the opportunity to move forward twice. The first time, I was filling a slot for our brigade executive officer while we attended the pre-command course. I was there for almost two months. As I spoke about in the previous chapter, I came back to the states for R&R, but for a much longer time than the regular R&R period. I was already looking forward to going back because I enjoyed being with our soldiers. I just never imagined what was about to happen.

1 March 2009, I was promoted to the rank of major. I was beyond excited. I had been waiting for that moment to be amongst the other majors that were already downrange. What happened next changed the whole next phase of my life. That following week, my mom suffered from a stroke. She was one of the healthiest humans I have ever known. She didn't smoke. She barely drank. She never ate processed foods. She was a jogger and a coffee drinker. She was not supposed to have this happen to her. She moved from California to Texas to help us with the kids during our first deployment. She purchased a house. She changed her life. So why in the F did this happen to her? I had no answers and didn't know how to deal with it. Have you ever written an angry text? That is how I feel right now as I type this. My fingers are pushing the keys even harder as I think about that whole month of March and beyond. I was not in a good place, but I am so damn grateful for the people who took care of the things that I should have been a part of.

I was set to go back to Afghanistan after that R&R but postponed it by two weeks. I could have stayed back entirely. They didn't need me. I chose to go back, and it was because I didn't know how to deal with all this shit. I was so conflicted. I was so angry. I was full of so many emotions. My brother took the wheel from there. Between my brother, husband, and father-in-law, they took care of the next steps to make sure my mom was taken care of. The feeling of what had just happened to my mom made me sick. I had to get out of there. Running away was the only way at the time. I can feel the judgment or maybe even a gasp coming from you right now, but trust me, I lived with that guilt for the longest time.

As soon as I got downrange, I had to get my mind right as best as I could. I buried myself in work and working out. If that wasn't enough, I even tried claiming my mom as a dependent so that I could provide for her — but I was denied twice by the military. I had many stressors and tried to remember what I told my soldiers back in 2005 when we first deployed to Iraq. We were supposed to have our game faces on. We were supposed to focus on the mission and not so much on what was going on back home. This was not the case for me, and I felt like a hypocrite.

The only thing that kept me somewhat sane was knowing that my mom was in good hands back home. If needed, we could figure out how to financially support her. We could figure out what the next steps were for her. Unfortunately, the best thing was to have her move in with my brother in California. That continues to weigh heavy on my heart. He took on one of the most difficult roles that I couldn't take on, and that was to take care of our mother. It was not only because I was deployed. It was also because I was not settled in one place yet. She needed a stable environment with consistent medical care access. I was not in the position to provide that for her.

So there I was, deployed to Afghanistan, a place where we were having battles all around us. My second time over there was for a different position. I was now a part of the redeployment operations. I assisted with making sure we had everything set in place to safely bring us back home. Although I can't really give all the details on what that entailed, just know that it is never an easy task. There are multiple layers and people involved. It is not as easy as just getting back on the plane.

Our day-to-day operations always included meetings. We had to come together to make sure we were all on track with all that was going on. Being behind the scenes brought my attention to things that I never thought I would have encountered. And yet, for some reason, I wanted to keep doing more. I asked our commander if I could go on a FOB recon with him. This was a FOB visit, so to speak. We had soldiers in about nine outlying locations. They were all doing things that our community never knew about. We took for granted the things that they couldn't have. Visiting those soldiers brought so much pain but also joy to my heart. They were truly serving our country in ways that we truly will never understand.

We lived on a small base located on an airfield. We could not leave unless it was for a mission. At times, it was depressing. One of the great things was having a gym and an airstrip to run on. It was at this very airstrip where I completed my first half marathon. The gym was a great escape to decompress, and it happened almost daily. I really appreciated having this space because it served us when we needed it the most.

We also had options like Pizza Hut® and Green Beans Coffee. It was actually pretty brilliant. It may seem like something trivial, but even the smallest of treats is so needed at times. I became addicted to the small things like their amazing iced tea and sugar cookies. I actually looked forward to it in the middle of the day or at night when coming off of a shift. It was like having a care package arrive. We really do appreciate everything that is sent.

One of my favorite things was the interaction we were able to have with some of the locals. On certain days of the week, right across the airfield, there would be a bizarre. It was an open area of local vendors selling their goods. I discovered the most beautiful marble pieces made into vases, bowls, and figurines shaped into animals. Over time, I purchased several to bring back home with me to have as something memorable of the good that was still left in Afghanistan.

We built relationships and were invited to eat with the locals. That was a huge deal for me, and I didn't know what to expect. They were friendly, and their food was amazing. Fresh bread, roasted chicken, and rice was one of their favorite dishes. It sounds like something we would eat at home, but it was certainly not made the same. Maybe it was something about the experience that made it that more special. It certainly will be remembered as a small part of history for myself and the soldiers that participated.

This deployment was certainly more difficult than the first one. I was so grateful to my cousins Kim and George for sending me emails with a rundown of my favorite shows that I was missing back home. Some of my favorites were *American Idol*, *Dancing with the Stars*, *Desperate Housewives*, *Private Practice*, and *Grey's Anatomy*. Kim would literally send me recaps of what happened in email format without missing a beat. I was always looking forward to reading those. Their words of encouragement and praise for how proud they were of me for continuing to do what I loved meant more to me than they ever knew. George (a.k.a. "Georgie") was a huge military supporter as he, himself, was part of the National Guard earlier in his life, and I didn't even know it until after he passed. When Georgie passed last year, it destroyed many of us. He helped me get through a lot of this deployment during and after as he knew I was struggling. I hope that, as he reads this from above, I am making him proud. Part of this is for you, Georgie.

We lost many soldiers during this rotation. I had never encountered this type of experience before. Being in the background and hearing of another lost, either by ground or air, made me feel emotions that were uncontrollable.

Before I deployed, I participated in the Army ten-miler with some of our amazing military spouses. While I was in D.C., our rear detachment sergeant major was also there. We had the privilege of visiting one of our wounded soldiers that were being treated at Walter Reed Medical Center. Seeing this soldier and knowing why he was there was even more reason for why I felt like I wanted to do more.

I specifically remember at least two incidents that have stuck with me. Although I mention these two, it doesn't negate the others that were lost. During this deployment, the unit also lost over thirty soldiers. We remember each and every one of them every year. Some of my peers worked directly with them. Some of us knew of them. They are not forgotten, and they never will be. These two specific incidents hit me hard because I remember being in the operations center when they happened.

We lost a soldier on foot patrol. We had been following his movements, and then it happened. He was gone. I didn't personally know him, but I knew of him. I was so angry. It consumed me. I left the TOC pissed off and emotional. I couldn't and didn't want to be around anyone. I changed and went immediately to the gym. My eyes filled with tears, and my thoughts started to fill with the question, *"Why are we even here?"* We had a chaplain to speak with, but no one could say anything or make sense of why this was happening. I immediately thought of their families and then my own.

The other incident that broke my heart happened to one of our dual-military married soldiers. Both she and her husband were deployed but in separate companies under the same brigade. The unit was following their actions as well. There will be times where you will make the best decision you see fit at that moment. Sometimes it does not always go the way it was planned. We lost two more soldiers that day, and she had to be notified that one of them was her spouse. My heart stopped for her. Being on a small base like ours forges stronger bonds. Our soldiers were very close and able to be there for her. That moment brought some of us to a standstill. *What just happened?* I don't think I will ever fully comprehend it, but the ones who were closest to them will have that ingrained into their hearts forever.

My late uncle served in this same division years prior, so I was proud to have been able to serve in it as well. It was yet another family legacy that I didn't know about until many years into my adult life. I felt honored to be there. I always felt like I needed to do more — even at the expense of my emotional wellbeing. I had no idea how that mindset was going to affect me. I had no other identity except for who I was in uniform. I had this idea in my head that I needed to feel validated. I can't speak for everyone else, but just speaking with those that I have, it seemed like that thought process was a common theme. Who were we if we were not deployed with our soldiers? Who were we out of uniform?

———

As if the losses abroad weren't enough, the first shooting at Fort Hood happened just a few months after I came back from that deployment. This next section is directly from the journal that I kept during that time.

5 November 2009
Loss

What else could possibly add fuel to the fire? The event happened on 5 November 2009 where Army officer Major Nidal Malik Hasan went on a shooting rampage on the Fort Hood military base at the in-processing center. Not many knew that I was short of ten minutes from being inside that building at the same time it happened. I was on my way there until a phone call saved me from what took place inside that building.

It was during the lunchtime hour that I was about to leave until I got a phone call. My Army sister needed a ride to pick up her car from the dealership maintenance shop. On the way there, we ran into heavy traffic trying to get off-post. I am not going to lie; I was irritated and wondering why it was taking so damn long to leave the installation. We were almost to the dealership when we got the call not to return because there was a shooting. They called us for accountability purposes. We were on the way out of the gate, sitting in the car when we saw police cars and ambulances streaming in. We started to get concerned when we were made aware of the details surrounding the situation.

Our unit was located right down the street from the Soldier Readiness Processing site. Who could have known? We tried calling our husbands, but they were unreachable. The whole post was on lockdown. The units were expediently trying to account for all of their Soldiers. For the parents that were on lockdown, they were not able to pick up their kids. Daycare centers were staying open late due to accommodating the families affected.

I was racing to get to my kids to bring them home. I was in shock from what had just taken place — even more so because I was just minutes from being in the building at the same time as when so many lives were lost.

I will never forget that day of the Fort Hood Massacre that left thirteen people dead and more than thirty wounded.

Survivors' guilt hit some of us really hard. I was not personally on a mission with any of our soldiers who passed, but I was there in the background, watching and praying. I was not on patrol, but I was there amongst our leaders, but I was there in the background, making sure that they had what they needed. I was not next to them when they were wounded, but I was in the background, hoping that they would make it through.

Sleepless nights, loss of appetite, nightmares, angry outbursts, daydreaming, sadness, and depression — these were just some of the things that some of us experience and/or continue to experience when coming back from an environment similar to this. This is what a deployment can do to you. And unless you knew how to talk about it, no one would ever really know what's going on. We were assigned to an infantry unit. We did not have time to show these emotions. *How did everyone else deal with these emotions?* It seemed as though we walked around like zombies. Some of us smiled, and some of us didn't. We grabbed our coffee, went into the meetings, came out of the meetings with our assigned tasks, and went straight to work. *How were we supposed to process all of this?* I have no idea. I understand that we all process our feelings differently. I just wish one of us would have spoken up and admitted to the fact that this was killing us all on the inside. That it was OK to be upset or sad or mad. I don't remember ever being able to freely say that. Nonetheless, I still looked up to our leaders and admired how strong they seemed on the outside. I tried so hard to be like them, but it only lasted for so long.

For those of you reading this, if we worked together in any capacity, know that I admired your courage, your bravery, and your ability to keep showing up and leading us. I don't know how you did it, but I saw it. This deployment broke many of us in different capacities. I have mixed feelings when I'm asked if I regret going. It changed me as a person. It changed the way I handled tough situations. It changed my relationships. It changed my family. It changed how I communicated if I chose to communicate at all. I was a disaster and thought that I could handle it all. I had no concern for what was happening at home. It was not like I was a heartless bitch, but I was in my own world. I got lost in a wave of emotions that made me blind to what was in front of me.

So, how do we come back from this? We surround ourselves with positivity. We find that person or tribe who is trying to bring you back to reality. Listen to them. I mean, really listen to them when they tell you that they have seen a change in you. Be open-minded to change. Not all change is bad. Find that inner voice and use it. Use it to speak your peace. Use it to save your life. Use it to communicate and ask for help. Stand up for yourself. No one else is going to do it for you. Unfortunately, there is only one of us. In the military, we are just a number — but at home, we are someone's parent, friend, sibling, spouse, and so much more beyond that.

Do not let what you cannot control consume you. This may all be easier said than done, but I am now here to tell you that it is possible. Believe in that higher power and let them guide you to the path that you are meant to be on. Open your eyes and ears, and make room for what is yours.

You can and will survive this. It will take work. It will suck. It will be hard. It will be worth it.

I am here, and I see you.

8: HOME

2009 – 2014, FORT HOOD, TEXAS | FORT LEAVENWORTH, KANSAS | EL PASO, TEXAS

I WAS BACK FROM MY second and last deployment. I was obviously not the same person I was when I went over there, but I had to look at what was ahead — my military career and my family.

There were many ugly bumps in the road that needed to be worked on. Many of them were due to my irrational behaviors. I was not a good person, and it is very difficult to admit that. I say this because it is true, and I have worked tirelessly at finding myself and becoming a better version of myself. Just like when I started my blog, if you didn't know me then, you will know a part of me now. I had many personal and professional battles to overcome. It was a long road, but all I had left was to keep trying.

Towards the end of 2009, I moved to a house around the corner. My husband and I shared visitation with the kids and had to focus on what was to come next. This was the year where I had my first panic attack. This was the year I had to get help and dig deep into what the hell was going on inside my head and heart. This was possibly one of the worst times in my life. I felt like I was living in a blur.

I knew what was happening, but I questioned why I let it happen. I lost myself and needed to get back before I lost anything else. There are some details that I purposely left out of this book for the privacy of my family.

Our next big professional move was to attend a course called Intermediate Level Education (ILE), also known as the Command General Staff College (CGSC), located at Fort Leavenworth, Kansas. It was an advanced-level education for those who were promoted to the rank of major or even a senior-ranking captain in all the military services. The schooling or the "school house" was composed of all the branches of the military to include those coming from abroad. It was a leadership school preparing us for what was next in our careers. It was over a ten-month period and pretty much kicked my ass. I was never very good in academics, and this was full of all the things that I had not done since college — a lot of reading and writing and sleepless nights.

During this time, my husband and I were separated and resided in two houses. While I never really shared this publicly, it was for good reason. I was ashamed. I was embarrassed. I was a pure wreck and just trying to get my shit together. I was also trying to protect the family. Sometimes, people don't need to know all of your shit. I just shared things about myself and kept my family out of it for the most part. Life still had to go on, and we had to be parents to our six-year-old son and nine-year-old daughter.

We agreed to live in side-by-side houses on-base. We wanted it to be as simple as we could for the kids. We continued to make decisions together when it came to the kids. We had to, somehow, get through this schooling so that we could progress to the next phase. It was going to be one hell of a challenge.

There were many firsts during this assignment, and I was trying to do the best I could, given the circumstances. We were fortunate to live half a mile from their elementary school. My daughter got her first flip phone at the age of nine because they were about to be latchkey kids. I was so stressed out at the fact that she and my son would be walking to and from school on their own for a few days a week, depending on our class schedule. Nonetheless, this mom was stressed out and always praying that the kids were OK on their own. I wasn't ready to give up that kind of control. Due to the reception in our building, our phones wouldn't work. I immediately switched phone carriers so that I was able to be in constant communication with the kids. It might sound trivial, but not having the phone work in the building that we spent eight hours in every day was not going to work for me.

Being back in a school environment was hard. Some days it really sucked. I felt the pain of staying up late working on papers and keeping up with the reading, all while still having to care for our six- and nine-year-old kids. The last time we were in this environment was when we were attending our training at Fort Leonard

Wood seven years prior. I tried to keep up the grind. I tried to stay on top of things, but when it came between choosing to spend time with the kids or reading those fifty pages, I chose the latter. The next day, I would wake up early to try and play catch-up. I would walk into class, barely awake and not ready for the day at all. There were days where I didn't think I was going to make it. I made very good friends who helped me along the way and gave me the short version of what our assignment was about. The thing I loved the most was the camaraderie we had in our small class. We looked out for each other and became a family. On the days when I needed them, they came through. Dual-military life was rough, and this was one of the times that it was surely tested.

After a few months, something snapped. I felt the pressure weighing on me with life, marriage, kids, parenting, and school. Something inside of me kept me from being able to keep up, and I broke. It was 24 August 2010 when another sign of my depression punched through the roof. It was my daughter's tenth birthday, and we were supposed to take her bowling. I had a mental breakdown and locked myself in the house. The kids tried so hard to figure out what was wrong with me. I couldn't speak and shut everyone out. I lay on the couch and slept as if nothing was wrong. I used the excuse that I wasn't feeling well and argued my way into staying home. I didn't think it was a big deal at the time. What I was thinking was that the kids were young and that they wouldn't remember. That was not the case. I learned just two years ago how much that day really impacted my daughter.

What we often forget as parents is that our children are always watching and listening. It took me years to finally realize that it took a while to hear it from them. They mimic us, and they carry on what we teach them. Watching both of my kids grow up, it is amazing to see their traits, characteristics, and mannerisms. It is scary how much they are just like us.

Now that we have learned how to have the hard conversations, I have learned a lot from the kids. I learned just how much they were scared of me when I had my angry moments. They didn't know how to deal with me. My daughter would confide in her dad and tell him that she thought I was bipolar. This really stung and hurt my feelings. I had no idea that the kids ever really thought about why I was so angry. I was consumed by my own self-loathing, my pain, and the feelings of how no one understood how I felt.

My father-in-law is a big gun collector, and for Christmas, he gifted me a beautiful 38 revolver with a mother of pearl handle. I can't remember the exact details of that day, but I know that I had the gun in my hand and was crying. My husband saw me, asked me what I was doing, and took it out of my hand. That was the last time I ever saw the revolver again. It was time. I needed help. But when was I going to be strong enough to get it? I had to get through school. I had to make it through. There was no failing out of this one. To even be given the opportunity to be there was rare. I could not let whatever was going on in my head affect me from graduating and progressing in my career. I pushed myself aside once again.

————

We did it. We graduated from ILE, and our next assignment was Fort Bliss in El Paso, Texas. I was given amazing leadership opportunities there. I also quickly learned that I needed to ask for help. I couldn't do everything on my own. I never wanted to ask someone to take care of my kids because my work hours were at odd times, and I didn't want to put that on anyone. It was different than when we were at Fort Leonard Wood because they were still babies then, and I had to place them in daycare — but since then, I have always figured out how to balance work and childcare. However, the next assignment that I accepted and desperately wanted required me to hire a nanny. I was devastated because I felt like I had failed. I felt weak. This may seem silly to you, but to me, it was crucial that I tried to always put my kids first when I was not in the field or on a deployment. I never imagined having to have someone else transport the kids to and from school.

Let me be clear, I do not discredit my fellow brothers and sisters who took the smart route and hired an au pair. I just never pictured myself going that route. Although I never did hire an au pair, I did go through four nannies before finding the right one that we were comfortable with. It definitely hurt my pride, but at this point in my career, I knew what had to be done.

My husband and I were still living in two separate houses and just a few blocks apart. We alternated weekends, and we supported each other's career paths. You know what happened? My kids became more resilient. They became stronger. We became a stronger team for it. It was never easy, but regardless of what was going to happen, we decided to communicate as best as possible and keep growing as individuals — all while raising our children the best way we knew how.

Toward the end of my assignment at Fort Bliss, it was time for my husband to relocate, and the only option at the time was to go to Korea on his own for an unaccompanied tour. For reasons outside of our control, my military branch could not send me to Korea with him. It was just more difficult to go as it would have required me to stay there for three years since I would be bringing the kids. It was much easier for him to go for the year on his own. Unfortunately, the kids were used to the separation. It didn't mean that it was any easier, but we knew what we had to do.

The kids and I stayed in El Paso, where my daughter started her first year of high school. Both of the kids have always attended either a small school or a faith-based school. It was just something that we had agreed on. For my daughter's first year of high school, I applied for her to attend an early college high school. I had heard good reviews about it and felt that it would be a very good environment for her. She had been doing very well academically and enjoyed school. Little did my husband and I know that this would be the time when she would grow up faster than we had anticipated, and we were most definitely not prepared. That may have been one of the most challenging times as parents, especially with one of us being away at any given time.

We navigated the best way we could. I admit the stress took over, and I started drinking. I used the famous words, "I don't have a problem." I really felt like I didn't. Looking back at those times, both of the kids admitted that they thought I did. It was noticeable enough that they spoke about it but not to the point where they told anyone. They both remember me drinking bottles at a time, whereas I only remember drinking a couple of glasses at a time. Nonetheless, they noticed — they thought it was not normal, and that was enough to make me regret getting myself into that hole. I should have known when I started putting wine into my coffee cups. Again, I didn't think there was a problem. I don't remember when I stopped drinking like that, but I did eventually stop. I didn't like the way it made me feel. I didn't like the jitters or the high it gave me. It was something that I couldn't control, so I stopped before it got to be much more than I could handle.

I loved my job. I loved being a leader. I loved working with the soldiers and the command team, which consisted of the command sergeant major (CSM), the battalion commander, and the battalion executive officer (XO). I learned what type of commander I wanted to be if I was given that opportunity. This was the second-most important leadership role in my career. It was something that I had aspired to work towards, and it happened. The first was being a company commander and the second one was to be an XO.

I had two commanders during my two years in this leadership position. The first one was a hard-charging female. I am not going to lie — it was so humbling working for her. I learned a lot, but it was also rough. I knew right off the bat that I was going to have to up my game. I respected her position and her journey through the ranks. I had never worked for another female before, so I quickly learned how I needed to act. Working for males for the first fourteen years of my career hardened me a lot. Working for a female made it a little worse. I felt like I was walking on pins and needles. I am not saying that she was a bad leader. I am grateful for my experience with her. I understand that some female leaders needed to be a little more aggressive in order to survive in a male-dominated profession. Because of the challenging environment, I had to learn how to ask for help with the kids. This is where I worked even harder to show her that I could handle the job.

The next commander was completely different. I learned how to truly work in a team. He trusted me. He gave me the confidence I needed and wanted to realize that I had the potential to keep going in my career. I will forever be grateful for what I learned from him. He was the type of leader I wanted to be and gave me even more drive to work towards becoming a battalion commander. That is now how it worked out in the end, but he left a lasting impression on me.

The last year and a half in El Paso were hard. I was given another opportunity to be an XO for the readiness unit that was responsible for training incoming soldiers that were scheduled to deploy overseas. It was an amazing learning experience, but the environment was a trying one. I only served for one year in that role and was sent to the unit that we fell under. It was a brigade-sized element that was the overhead for the readiness unit. I have never wanted out of a unit as much as I did this one. I decided that if I didn't do something about my depression, I was not going to make it. I decided to seek counseling. The problem is that I did not want anyone to know. I already felt like I didn't belong. I knew that this was temporary because I was set to move; we just didn't know where yet. My husband was still in Korea and was waiting to find out if and where he would be taking battalion command. The waiting game was stressful as hell.

One of the challenges of being dual-military is that the Army needs to find jobs for the both of us. Sometimes, it is not always in the same location. We were very fortunate to have been able to be stationed together, except for when he had to go to Korea unaccompanied. For the most part, we were on the same base or within thirty minutes of each other. This is not always the case for dual-military families. I would often state that I had some kind of medical appointment but instead went to a therapist. I hated being at that duty assignment. The environment was toxic. I went as far as calling the branch manager who worked on our follow-on assignments and asked him to get me the hell out of there. At this point, I really didn't care.

Of all the places that I kept putting last on my list to PCS throughout my whole Army career, guess where we ended up? Fort Polk, Louisiana. I truly feel now that God knew all along what was supposed to be. He had a method to the madness that we didn't want to see. We embraced the suck and ended up loving every minute of it.

Read on to see how Louisiana ended up being one of our least-desired yet most rewarding experiences in our careers.

9: INSIDE THE WIRE

Inside the Wire — Inside an enemy combatant detention facility. Working "inside the wire" of the enemy combatant detention facility can lead to stress for U.S. troops working here.[10]

28 SEPTEMBER 2015 – 29 DECEMBER 2016, FORT POLK, LOUISIANA

This chapter is directly from my journal entries during the time I retired. Although I could have put it into a more story-like format, I kept it this way so you can see my exact thought process and emotions during this time.

———

Sept 28, 2015

I have been wanting to write for a very long time. It started in journals. Random thoughts about feelings and such. I have seen others use this site and never really thought I could do it until now. Tonight. At 2110. I am older now. Much wiser. Have gone through a lot of shit. Life happened. I am now forty years old. I have been in the Army for over sixteen years. I have two amazing and resilient children: a fifteen-year-old daughter and a twelve-year-old son. I could not have made it this far without them.

Life happened, and now I am here at Fort Polk, LA. Life happened, and now I am walking on thin ice, waiting to see if the Army will decide to keep me in. If they think I am suitable enough. If they think I can still do this. Through tears and anger, I have learned the hard way that a piece of paper cannot and will not ever define who I am. Life happened, and I made mistakes. I used my heart instead of my head.

Do I regret this life? No. It's been hard. "It's OK," I tell myself. God has a bigger plan for me. Deep inside, I am trying to make myself feel like it will be a relief if I don't stay in. Who am I kidding? I love soldiers. I am almost there. I can retire in four years! No. I need to think positively, but I also need to face reality. It's OK. I will be fine. Tonight I will go to sleep and look forward to another day with my amazing leaders, my amazing team, and the fact that they actually value what I bring to the fight. Tonight I will be thankful. Goodnight, my sweets. Let's start this week off right. Until tomorrow...

––––––––

Sep 29, 2015

I firmly believe that everything happens for a reason, regardless if that reason is unexpected or they end up hurting you beyond what you could ever imagine. I have experienced the good, the bad, and the ugly. At some point in my life, my heart hurt so bad that I never thought I would recover, but I did. I lost my way for a long time. I thought, "I got this." "I am strong enough." "I can make my own decisions." "I'm good." Well, I wasn't.

Then, one day, something happened. Something came over me, and I found my way again. I can't explain it, but I obviously needed it. No, I'm still not perfect, and, yea, I still have my days. But, I am definitely not where I was six years ago or even three years ago. I have come to realize that I have a strong support system. I have amazing kids, loving friends, soldiers who look up to me, and family I adore. I love to see them all grow and prosper in their lives.

I am blessed.

I still make mistakes, yes, because I feel. I love hard. I care. I am human. I know that I have God, and I have people in my life who are always there. I look at my kids and say to myself, "Wow, I am their mom, and they need me." It's still hard to believe that these "little" people are just like their dad and me. They see how we react to things. How we deal. How we move on. We are the ones who teach them about life. I have to ask myself, "How do I want them to live their life?" not as I did back then, but as I am doing now. I understand that they will make their own mistakes, but I also want them to learn that they can recover from them as well, that I made it through, and so can they. We make sure to tell them how much we love them every single day. It's the little things that count.

I am blessed.

I wouldn't change a thing because those mistakes are who I am. Negative or positive, my experiences are what have made me who I am today. Now it's time to be the best parent I can.

I am blessed, and I am grateful.

October 5, 2015

I know that I am not alone when I say that there are days when I am just overwhelmed with life. Day-to-day things, like who's going to take the kids to and from school, what's for dinner, who's going to make dinner, and then... oh, yeah, we ran out of milk. Gah!! Sometimes I just hate going grocery shopping. It just seems like it's a never-ending cycle. But we can't live off of pizza, and I refuse to keep eating out. Thank God the kids can do their own laundry and make their own lunches because being a soldier and a mom is tough at times, and any little bit helps. I can see why my peers hire au pairs to live with them. I had a nanny at my last duty station — went through four as a matter of fact — but it was only because my job was so demanding. I didn't ask her to do anything except take the kids to school and pick them up. Sometimes when I was going to be late, she did make them dinner, but I tried to not make that a habit. I just couldn't bring myself to hiring an au pair to come love in my house. I don't know how people do it, but I do understand why they do it. So I am going to try and get back in the habit of cooking on Sundays or at least prep the meals. It's a start.

My mom has been here for the past three months, and she did it all. We. Were. Spoiled. Today was the first day of, "What are we doing to do without her?" hence why the Sunday cook/prep has begun. It was quite humorous. I even got the kids involved so that they can learn how to make this a team effort and to teach them how to cook — life lessons. So now I'm in bed at 2050 and have to be up by 0445 to begin my week. It's OK, though, because I get to see soldiers, and they make it worth the early and hectic days. This life has its ups and downs, but I don't think that I would change a whole lot about it.

Until tomorrow...

Dec 8, 2015

What the hell, hormones? You are seriously killing me. I am crying at almost anything and everything. Went to bed at 1930. No dinner. No appetite. Not cool. Life. Mom. Soldier. Friend. No one can take that away, but lately, it's been my heart. How do I shut that part off? I would like to know. Any recommendations are appreciated.

June 10, 2016

And so it began… What I never thought would come this far, has. I actually survived being an Army soldier for about seventeen years. My plan was three years, then get the hell out. Nope. Every year I was undecided. I never really had a plan. I was one of those special officers who just took it year by year. So, honestly, I am surprised I made it this far. I desperately wanted to make it to twenty years.

I was terrified of what was to come after retirement. I wanted the promotion but was tired of waiting. I was a mess. When the boards convened, I was sick to my stomach, hoping and praying for just one more year. Everything had gotten more competitive. I kept thinking about all the times I could have done better. Could have cared more. Could have been a better leader etc. etc. Well, it was a little too late. Here I am now with four months left because "The Army is downsizing," also known as putting out good leaders. Or it was just my time.

Yes, I was pissed, angry, resentful. But now I realize that it is my time. Sure, questions have been asked about why I can't stay in. "Isn't there something I can do?" No, there isn't. I am, along with a few other peers, in a hurry to be out, like, hurry up, get your shit together, you are gonna either retire or get a severance pay kind of deal. Yup, it sucks. But, here I am. I am loved. I am supported. I have people on my team. I had a good ride. My life has been wild with ups and downs, loves, hates, and regrets, but they have made me, and I have survived. I am now here to help others. This is a new beginning to the end of another chapter.

Dec 29, 2016

It's been a while since I last wrote anything here. Life happened. I have spent the last seven months rushing to get my life situated for what the hell I was going to do after the Army.

25 May 2016 is when I found out that I had, yet again, not made the promotion list to the next rank of lieutenant colonel.

No promotion meant retirement.

All my Army career, I never knew what I wanted to do or be. I took it year by year. Some days it sucked, and some days I loved it so much it hurt. I made sacrifices. I made poor decisions (some being food-related). But deep inside, I wanted this promotion so bad. When I didn't make the list the first time, I was heartbroken. I cried, and then I prayed, and then I left it up to the big man upstairs. I had visions. I had dreams. I received inspirational words from friends and family. I just knew this would be it. I was going to make it this time. I. Just. Knew. It.

Then I got the notification from my boss (who is now a dear friend). He hugged me. Said he was sorry. I held back the tears, sent a text to one of my good friends, and just sat at my desk. My friend then called and asked if I was OK. I let it all out. I walked to the bathroom and sat on the floor. I cried. I was pissed. Why me? Why not me? I needed this. I felt like a failure. I regretted all the bad decisions I made. What if I would have tried harder? Why didn't I hire an au pair as all my other friends did? I should have considered that option so that I had help to watch my kids. Instead, I drowned myself in work. Why did I go through five nannies? I was filled with so many emotions. The "what ifs" were clouding my mind.

It took me a week to get the fact that I didn't make the list through my system. I started seeing all the social media posts of friends getting promoted. I was so freaking jealous yet proud of my friends' accomplishments. This shit was real, and it was hard. For seven months, I had to give up the life I had built over the past seventeen years and five months. Could they be any crueler? I mean, really.

My award was shit. I refused to attend the retirement ceremony, but here we are. As of 1 November 2016, I am retired, with two ID cards and everything. Still no job because I was tired of working just to work. I want to make a difference now. I want to do what I want. How the hell am I going to do that with no money? Yeah. And I still haven't received my retirement check.

So here I am. I've been drowning my sorrows in retail therapy. Clothes. Shoes. Now I am drowning in all the materialistic things that I did not need. Drawers are full. Closet is full. Still not happy. Go figure. It's like a drug. The thrill of getting something new and pretty… and now I don't want it. Trying to sell it is consuming my time. I need to reevaluate things. My credit card is freaking ridiculous. I was doing so good, and now I have to pay that shit off. How? Yeah…

So I'm back. It's time to wake up and realize that this new drug called Lularoe isn't fixing things. Pretty skirts and dresses aren't getting me a job or paying my bills.

Wake up, Annette. Snap out of it.

I'm back, and it's time to make some changes.

10: AAR

> *An After-Action Review (AAR) is a professional discussion of an event, focused on performance standards, that enables soldiers to discover for themselves What happened, Why it happened and How to sustain strengths and improve on weaknesses.*[11]

2013 – 2016, FORT POLK, LOUISIANA
2018 – PRESENT, FAIRFAX, VIRGINIA

HERE WE WERE at Fort Polk, Louisiana. This was the LAST place we ever wanted to go to in our military careers. Every time we were about to PCS, we were given a list of about ten places that were available. We were to rank them in order of where we would like to go, but nothing was ever promised. Some amazing things happened there, even though it was the last place on Earth that I had ever wanted to be. My husband was selected for battalion command, a position that is very competitive. After quite a few mishaps involving where I was supposed to be assigned, I was well-received in the section where I would spend my last two years in the Army.

I worked with a phenomenal team that was responsible for the posturing and training of incoming units for deployment. This included many briefings to the commanding general, late nights, early mornings, and a lot of running around like chickens with our heads cut off — basically, just like how most of my military career was like. I just didn't realize that I would be enjoying this type of pace for the last time within the walls of the Joint Readiness Training Center (JRTC) building. I worked with some outstanding leaders that I now consider my friends. We all felt the joy and pain together. We were truly a team, and I am immensely grateful that the last part of my career was spent here. God must have known what I would truly need during one of the most difficult times in my life.

I became really good friends with my boss and his family. His mother held a very special place in my heart, and her spirit still carries with me even after her passing. I used to care for her when he had to leave town. When she passed, it broke my heart as she was someone very special. I grew to care for her as though she were part of my family. I was so blessed to have been brought into their lives for a short period of time.

My boss had two Maltese dogs that brought me to my happy place. They had just had puppies, and he knew that I needed something to clear my mind. Little did I know that one of the puppies would be my saving grace. I named her Lulu, and I've loved her for the past four years. She has been my everything since the day I brought her home. I had three other dogs at the time, and adding a fourth was against the base's policy. I just knew that I needed her and brought her home anyway. If you have a pet, then you know how much joy they bring you — especially during the most trying of times. It is pretty amazing how much they can sense what you are feeling. Lulu saved me from myself through the tears and thoughts of wanting to give up everything completely. There was something special about her that made me want to continue to live.

I was given three different options of how I would like to end my career and thirty days to make that decision. I sought out an Army recruiter to look at options of how I could finish the last three or more years. I didn't realize how hard it was going to be. I was given six months to get my affairs in order and be ready to no longer wear this uniform. I was angry.

Just months prior, I had been trying to prepare myself for this exact situation, but I still had hope. I prayed and hoped that all of the sacrifices, struggles, and obstacles would have, somehow, paid off with this promotion. I was left feeling like I did it for nothing. I was filled with disappointment when I left the recruiter's office. After having that hard conversation, it did not make sense to continue my service but instead take the option to retire. I was just not ready to stop being who I thought I was supposed to be. MAJ Whitt.

I spent the whole thirty days in deep reflection. I spoke to other peers and even civilians to get some feedback on what they thought I could do once I was out of the only career I knew. Nothing was promised, and nothing looked promising. I chose to retire early and take some time to figure my life out again.

I was given six months to prepare for one of the biggest changes in my life. What was also difficult to accept was that I was only given six months versus the one year that most retirees are given. The first thought that crossed my mind was, *"How in the hell am I supposed to figure out the rest of my life in six months when I have just spent the last seventeen years in that same process?"* This was so unfair. I was pissed off at the world.

I tried to get through those months as best as I could. I continued to show up to work and formations and completed the assigned tasks that I didn't feel comfortable passing off due to my guilt. I hated giving someone a task that I could do myself. I still couldn't quite grasp that, as each day passed by, it put me closer to the end of what I had known for over seventeen years. I didn't know how to do this.

I attended the Transition Assistance Program (TAP program). I personally felt like it could have been filled with a lot more information than a general overview. Trying to write a résumé in a day was mentally impossible. I felt like there could have been an option of classes based on career paths. The amount of time we spent on being provided with dozens of websites and phone numbers and trying to learn how to dress could have been well-spent talking about the mental health aspect of our transition. No one spoke about how difficult it was going to be when we no longer wore the uniform that defined us. Or at least, that is how it felt to many of us. It took me over three years to finally be at peace and learn that a piece of paper and a uniform didn't define who I was as a person. I was much more than camouflage.

I was very bitter and couldn't get myself in the mindset needed for this transition.

I stopped caring and went through the motions when it came to out-processing certain sections of the base. I had to go to the ID card section to turn in my active duty card for a retiree one. I had to go to Finance to change my pay status. I was no longer a Major or an O-4. I was now a retiree. I no longer had that rank that I had been holding onto for the past seven years. Who was I now?

A retirement ceremony was held every month for all of the retiring soldiers on Fort Polk. I decided not to attend the one that was supposed to include me. I received emails, questions, and calls about it. I literally wanted nothing to do with the Army. I am not proud of my behavior nor my attitude, but at that moment, I felt like I didn't deserve to be on that stage or be recognized. I was humiliated.

When I left the final office where I had to sign my name on the line saying that my service was complete, I was sitting in the chair behind the desk of the last person I saw that day. I was handed a box with the United States flag, a certificate of appreciation, and my DD214 (Certificate of Release or Discharge from Active Duty). I took the box and walked out of the building with a knot in my chest. *Was this really it?* I went to my car, sat in the seat, and cried. I cried so hard that I couldn't breathe. *What just happened?*

I drove home, took the uniform off, and sat on the couch. I didn't want to do anything or talk to anyone for as long as possible. I apologized to the kids because

I felt like I failed them. My daughter said, "It's OK. Mom. Now you will have more time with us." She was right, and I wanted to appreciate that — but it was still very difficult for me to process. I regretted not attending the ceremony if not for me but for them. I wanted the kids to be proud of me but was still too embarrassed. Although it has been four years since then, and my kids are, in fact, proud of me, I still carry that weight in my heart.

I was retired. I should have been as excited as some of my friends would have been. I, instead, wallowed in self-pity and didn't have a care in the world. The times that I should have been writing a résumé, I would sleep and binge-watch Netflix. I no longer had to show up for formation. I no longer had to carry around a second work phone. I no longer had to figure out how I was going to leave work to attend the kids' school activities or sports games. I should have been looking at this as a positive thing, and some days I did. On the other days, I felt lost and without a purpose. I had no idea what I was going to do next. It was not like I was not qualified. I had a freaking graduate degree! I was in the damn Army for over seventeen years. Why was I feeling so unaccomplished? Sadly, I was not the only one who felt like this. I needed to find something that I was passionate about, or I was going to lose my mind.

I tried to do things that I wasn't able to do before. I volunteered more. I became a brand ambassador for a company that I truly believed in and aligned with what I respected, Sword and Plough. I did an interview and discovery call and was accepted. That was something that I needed. I needed to feel validated again. Representing a woman-veteran-owned and -operated company that recycled military gear was something that I knew I wanted to be a part of. I have been with them for four years now and still believe in their mission.

I started and stopped five podcast episodes. I tried using that platform to share my struggles, but I now know that I was not in the right mindset quite yet. I knew that I needed to talk about it. I didn't know where or to whom, but my inner self needed to be let out. I was in contact with my former soldiers, and after some social media posts, we had the hard conversations that I didn't know how to have. I was hiding them with self-destruction. I had been holding onto decades' worth of trauma, and I was slowly fading. I hid so many parts of myself for fear of judgment. I slowly started losing the battle of being tough. I no longer had to cover up anymore. I was now able to let go but was terrified of doing so. I was the volcano that was slowly erupting.

After many conversations about how transitioning out of the military was, and is, difficult for so many, I knew that I needed to start talking about it more... But I had to start slow. I was not quite ready to fully jump in. I needed to ease into it because I was still afraid of what others might think. I created a WordPress account and started writing. I wrote until I was ready to voice my words to the world.

I was invited into a Facebook Group called Vetpreneur Tribe. Little did I know that joining this group would change the trajectory of my next four years. I met so many talented and amazing people that would end up changing parts of my life. If any of you are reading this, and you know who you are, I thank you from the bottom of my heart for saving me. Because of you, I fought to make this into a business to help others who are fighting the same fight. You are the tribe I never knew I needed.

I hired a veteran turned friend to create a website for me so I could start the blogging journey. He was recommended to me by someone who helped make her dream into reality. After seeing his work and speaking with him, I knew that he would also make my dream come true. I have told him several times how thankful I am for him, but I will say it again here — thank you from the bottom of my heart for turning my vision into a reality. I pressed the publish button, and it went live to the whole world. All the secrets that I had been hiding were now made public. I was absolutely sick to my stomach and second-guessing what I had just done. *What were people going to think? What were they going to say?*

The name came to me one day. Without hesitation, I named the website A Wild Ride Called Life. It couldn't have been more perfect. I found a woman on Etsy to design my logo, which would incorporate the California highway sign near the beach where I would often go as a teenager. I also added my dream car, the Volkswagen Bus. I have fond memories of my elementary school days and will always cherish the memory of my 6th-grade teachers, Mr. C and Mrs. H. Mr. C would always have his bicycle in the back of his VW Bus when he came to school. As I got older, I knew that one day I wanted to own a VW Bus, but with the constant moving with the military, I never was able to purchase one. When it came to creating my website and later turning it into a business, I knew that this was the opportunity to make a path of my very own. I couldn't be happier with what it has turned out to be and the people I have helped because of it. I never imagined sharing pieces of myself online and on a platform that I could be proud of.

I was diagnosed with depression, and I live with post-traumatic stress disorder (PTSD) and anxiety. I chose to use the word "live" instead of suffering because I know how it was consuming me and my life. After the car accident, I knew that I was given a chance at life for a reason. But what was I going to do with it?

———

How WAS I GOING TO turn my mess into my message?

How was I going to make all this shit into something positive?

I started speaking. I started writing. I started podcasting. I had no idea where it was going to go, but the most important thing is that *I started*. These past two years of living in Virginia have taught me to work on becoming a better version of myself. I learned to step outside of my comfort zone due to a lot of help from other entrepreneurs and coaches as well as my friends. I wanted people to know that they were not alone in their battles. I wanted to create a platform and a safe space where we can use our voices to share our stories. So, why not also start a podcast?

I created The Truths We Hide podcast on 21 Oct 2020, and it is still going. The truths we hide are battles that so many of us live with due to fear of judgment, embarrassment, and a whole laundry list of other words and feelings. I never imagined having guests who needed a place to share those stories of triumph. Listening and sharing raw and heartfelt stories from real people is the most heartwarming and heartbreaking thing I could ever do.

PEOPLE JUST WANT TO BE HEARD.

People also want to help other people.

I still have those days where I need to step away and breathe. I also have days where helping people lights a fire in my soul. After all this trauma and these hardships and life experiences, I am finally in a place where I know that I am making a difference. At the young age of forty-five, this is the time to keep going.

This life has been scary and challenging, and, as you all know by now, I didn't want to be here. But, by leaving this Earth, I would have never been able to start something so needed. If you find something that lights your soul on fire and it is your true passion, then do it! No matter how scary it is, keep doing it. Even if you fall, fail, or break, keep doing it. Never give up on something that you truly love — especially now. 2020 and part of 2021 have shown us things that we never expected to see in our world. It has also shown us things that we were meant to see. Whether you believe in the higher power or not, just open your heart and your eyes to see and accept what is here right now.

Ending the stigma on mental health and stopping suicide are just two reasons why I hope this book reaches you during your time of need.

There are party lights at the end of the tunnel, and I will be there waiting for you.

PART TWO

DIGGING DEEPER

WORKBOOK

DIGGING DEEPER

You can download a free, printable version of this guide on the "Book" page at www.awildridecalledlife.com.

I decided to create this workbook because, throughout the book, I shared all of my obstacles but didn't dig into how I overcame them. I do not want to focus on how long it took me, but rather the tools I used to get me here.

Here you will find some questions to ponder as you go back through the chapters. I invite you to print this off on the website or use this space here to take your own notes.

1: FALL IN

1. Have you ever experienced abandonment? When was your first experience?

_____

_____

2. How did this affect you? Do you feel that it has made you stronger?

_____

_____

3. How have you worked through the abandonment? What steps have you taken to gain back control of your life?

_____

_____

4. Did you confront the one who abandoned you? Did it bring you peace, and are you able to forgive them?

_____

_____

5. Where would you say you are in life right now? What words would you describe how you are feeling?

_____

_____

6. To help shift your mindset, try putting those words into phrases such as "I am stronger because," "I am still upset because," etc.

_____

_____

2: DRESS RIGHT, DRESS

1. Have you ever felt like you didn't belong and that you were trying to find your place in the world?

_____

_____

_____

2. Has this experience kept you from moving forward, or did it make you take charge of your life?

_____

_____

_____

3. If it kept you from moving forward, what are some steps that you feel you need to take to gain control today?

_____

_____

_____

4. If it made you want to take charge of your life, what steps could you share to help others?

_____

_____

_____

3: ROLL CALL

1. Trauma comes in many forms. It can be emotional, verbal, and/or physical. It can start as a child or well into your adult years. Have you experienced trauma?

   _____

   _____

2. The first thing I would like to tell you is that your experiences do not define you. The second thing is that it is not your fault! Write these sentences: "It was not my fault." "I will not let my trauma define me."

   _____

   _____

3. Has the trauma kept you from moving forward personally and/or professionally? What is keeping you from letting go? Write down some of those feelings (anger, resentment, ashamed):

   _____

   _____

   _____

4. How are you going to take your life back and not let the trauma take control? Start with some phrases like "I will not let the trauma take over," "I will not let it define me," etc.

   _____

   _____

5. How are you going to turn your mess into your message?

   _____

   _____

4: FARGO

1. Have you ever made a spur-of-the-moment, life-changing decision that you didn't put much thought into? What was it? What was the outcome?

   _____

   _____

   _____

   _____

2. When you made that decision, was it to prove something to yourself or someone else? How did those actions make you feel?

   _____

   _____

   _____

   _____

3. Have you ever regretted those decisions? OR do you feel like they were lessons learned? Briefly write down your thoughts about this. Would you have done anything differently?

   _____

   _____

   _____

   _____

5: SANDBOX

1. Have you experienced any major life changes that were out of your control? Was it for professional or personal reasons? How did you change your mindset in order to adjust?

   _____

   _____

   _____

   _____

2. How difficult was it to put your game face on? What steps did you take in order to focus on the current situation without letting distractions hinder it?

   _____

   _____

   _____

   _____

3. What was the most difficult challenge? Did you have a support system in place to help guide you through these challenges? How did they help you?

   _____

   _____

   _____

   _____

6: R&R

1. Think about a time in your life when you let yourself slip into a downward spiral. What were the circumstances? If you could go back, what would you do differently?

_____

_____

_____

_____

2. How do you handle stress? Write some things down like "I go for a run," "I watch TV," "I listen to music," etc.

_____

_____

_____

_____

3. Do you feel that you give yourself enough credit or grace for the things that go well?

_____

_____

_____

_____

7: BACK TO THE SANDBOX

1. How strong are your faith and/or spiritual beliefs? Do you believe in a higher power? How does that play into your life?

_____

_____

_____

_____

2. Do you have difficulty knowing or finding your worth? Do you lean into your faith to see that you are worthy and made for so much more than you think?

_____

_____

_____

_____

3. Have you ever felt like quitting? What are some of the things that help you to keep showing up?

_____

_____

_____

_____

8: HOME

1. Have you ever experienced a drastic change in your family dynamic? How did you handle it?

_____

_____

_____

_____

2. When you hit a low point in your life, do you pray about it? Do you use your faith to help navigate through those trying times?

_____

_____

_____

_____

3. Have you ever experienced a panic or anxiety attack? What are some of the tools you used to overcome it?

_____

_____

_____

_____

10: AAR

1. What are you grateful for? List them here.

_____

_____

_____

2. How do you help yourself to focus on positivity, truth, and hope?

_____

_____

_____

3. What brings you joy even on the hard days?

_____

_____

_____

4. What are some of your strengths, skills, or gifts? How are you using them? Which ones are you using the most?

_____

_____

_____

5. What legacy would you like to leave behind?

_____

_____

_____

AFTERWORD

Now that you have had the chance to go through this workbook, I would like to leave you with a few things to think about:

+ It is OK not to be OK; you are allowed to take a time out. You are allowed to set boundaries. You are allowed to say no. You have permission to put yourself first.
+ Your mess is your message. All the crap that you have been through was done for you and not to you. Read that again.
+ You were made for more. Yes, more than you can even imagine. Your past does not define you. Your mistakes do not define you. Your trauma does not define you. You are here for a reason, and your story is not over. This is just the beginning.
+ You are needed. You are wanted. You are a blessing to so many people, and I need you to remember that.
+ Always be you for you. Never be someone that you are not. Be someone that you love. Be someone that you are proud of. Be you for you and not for anyone else.
+ Bad days will happen, and that is OK. Bad days will turn into good days as long as you keep your head up high and smile at the

sky. Remember that you "get to" wake up each day. You "get" to do anything you want. Focus on that and appreciate the little things.

+ Mindset is everything. Mindset is everything. Mindset is everything.

Need more tips, tools, or motivation? Please contact me via my website! I am here for you.

REFERENCES

1. Polk County Publishing Company. "Six Injured in Multiple-Vehicle Crash." Tyler County Booster, August 27, 2018. https://www.tylercountybooster.com/index.php/news/2447-six-injured-in-multiple-vehicle-crash.

2. Farflex, Inc. "Fall in." The Free Dictionary. http://www.thefreedictionary.com/fall in.

3. Wikimedia Foundation, Inc. "Drill Command." Wikipedia. May 08, 2006. https://en.wikipedia.org/wiki/Drill_command.

4. EducationDynamics. "Aligning the Platoon in a Line Formation." Army Study Guide. https://www.armystudyguide.com/content/Drill_Sergeant_Resources/Drill_sergeant_presentations/aligning-the-platoon-in-a-2.shtml.

5. Dictionary.com, LLC. "Roll Call." Dictionary.com. https://www.dictionary.com/browse/roll-call.

6. Military Advantage. "Military Jargon from Iraq and Afghanistan." Military.com. https://www.military.com/join-armed-forces/military-jargon-from-iraq-and-afghanistan.html.

7. Teege. "Military Slang.docx." Scribd. January 5, 2020. https://www.scribd.com/document/441748560/Military-Slang-docx.

8. Wikimedia Foundation, Inc. "R&R (military)." Wikipedia. January 26, 2021. https://en.wikipedia.org/wiki/R%26R_ (military)#:~:text=R%26R%2C%20military%20slang%20for%20 rest,(no%20family)%20duty%20stations.

9. Hoffner, Sydnery. "23 Slang Terms Only Veterans Know." BestLife (blog), November 11, 2020. https://bestlifeonline.com/veteran-slang-terms/.

10. Hoffner, Sydnery. "23 Slang Terms Only Veterans Know." BestLife (blog), November 11, 2020. https://bestlifeonline.com/veteran-slang-terms/.

11. EducationDynamics. "After Action Review AAR (ArmyStudyGuide.com)." Army Study Guide. https://www. armystudyguide.com/content/powerpoint/Training_the_force_ presentations/after-action-review-aar-2.shtml.

ABOUT THE AUTHOR

Annette is a military spouse of 22 years, mother to a daughter, Haeli (20 yrs old; (college junior at Sam Houston State University) and son, Blaze (17 yrs old; high school senior at Robinson High School) and veteran who served in the Army for seventeen years and 4 months as a Chemical officer including a deployment to Iraq and Afghanistan.

Annette commissioned as a 2nd Lieutenant in the U.S. Army as a Chemical Officer from the ROTC Program at Arizona State University (Tempe, AZ). She has a B.A. in Psychology from Arizona State University and an M.S. in Environmental Management from Webster University.

She retired and decided to become an Accidental Entrepreneur to be able to make up for lost time with her children and use her voice to share her story about real life after the Army and living with mental illness. Since her retirement she has relocated from Fort Polk, LA to Fairfax , VA to support her husband's military career.

Her blog *A Wild Ride Called Life*®, LLC. incorporates stories from her post military life in which she shares how she lives life as being a mom and military spouse living with PTSD, anxiety and depression.

Along with writing, she also hosts a Podcast titled "The Truths We Hide" in which not only does she share her story, but she also has guests who share theirs and offers advice to others to help them know that they are not alone.

Annette is a mentor for veterans on Veterati and for military spouses on Ementor. Annette also has a passion for volunteering. Annette is a volunteer freelance writer for Association of Military Spouse Entrepreneurs. She volunteers as a mentor for TAPS, Tragedy assistance Program for children survivors, The American Foundation for Suicide Prevention and the Trauma Survivors Network.

You can check out more about Annette at the following:

linktr.ee/a_wild_ride_called_life

ABOUT THE PUBLISHER

TACTICAL 16

Tactical 16 Publishing is an unconventional publisher that understands the therapeutic value inherent in writing. We help veterans, first responders, and their families and friends to tell their stories using their words.

We are on a mission to capture the history of America's heroes: stories about sacrifices during chaos, humor amid tragedy, and victories learned from experiences not readily recreated — real stories from real people.

Tactical 16 has published books in leadership, business, fiction, and children's genres. We produce all types of works, from self-help to memoirs that preserve unique stories not yet told.

You don't have to be a polished author to join our ranks. If you can write with passion and be unapologetic, we want to talk. Go to Tactical16.com to contact us and to learn more.